Mediterranean plants and gardens

Le Vicomte de Noailles / Roy Lancaster

ISBN 0 903001 23 3

FLORAPRINT Ltd, CALVERTON, NOTTINGHAM

Front cover.
Villa Roquebrune,
a rich array of plants including *Solanum rantonensis*,
Lantana sellowiana, *Aeonium* and *Gazania* backed by cypress
and Aleppo pine

Contents

Acknowledgements

Vicomte de Noailles

Roy Lancaster

*We wish to express our gratitude to the
Vicomte de Noailles; he not only convinced us of
the interest which would be aroused
by a book on the plants of the Mediterranean coast, and
in particular the plants
of the Côte d'Azur, but he also willingly guided us
around the wonderful gardens and found
perfect specimens of plants for us to photograph.*

*Thanks also are due to the Vicomte de Noailles for his
help with the initial preparation of plant lists
and for his assistance in editing the manuscripts.
His knowledge of the subject matter is profound
and his wide experience is exemplified by positions
such as presidency of the
International Dendrological Society and the
vice-presidency of the Royal Horticultural Society.*

*We are certain that the Vicomte, in suggesting the
production of this book, had the generous
intention of offering to plant lovers a document which
sets out to make a definitive statement on what are,
or have been, the gardens of the Côte d'Azur.
We deeply regret the current take-over of the
countryside by construction work which leads to the
progressive disappearance of these gardens
created on the initiative of certain great plant lovers.*

*We are equally grateful to Roy Lancaster,
who agreed to collaborate in the creation of this book.
Roy Lancaster, curator of the Hillier Gardens
and Arboretum close to
Winchester in England, is known by a large public.
Besides his function as curator of
the Arboretum, he is a technical advisor and contributor
to several horticultural magazines, and publications.*

*Above all, Roy Lancaster has the gift of writing
particularly vivid text, proof that he lives with ana
for plants. He has taken part in several plant-hunting
expeditions to different parts of the world, and is the
youngest-ever recipient of the Royal Horticultural
Society's Gold Veitch Memorial Medal.*

*We wish to place on record our appreciation
of the help given to us by
Dr. Peter Raven, Director of the Missouri Botanical Garden,
who made valuable comments on Mediterranean climates
and their world distribution.
He also provided the basis for the maps on page 9,10.*

*Our thanks also to :
Madame Pierre Champin, La Chèvre d'Or, 06 Biot
Mrs. N. Warre, Villa Roquebrune, 06 Roquebrune, Cap Martin
Mr. Roderick Cameron,
Le Clos Fiorentina, 06 St Jean, Cap Ferrat
Madame A. Plesch, La Léonina, 06 Beaulieu s/Mer
Mr. A. Norman, La Garoupe, 06 Cap d'Antibes
who have, with great kindness, allowed us to take
photographs in their gardens.
Finally, an especially large thank-you must go to
Michael Warren, gallant photographer for our books
during the past few years, who has the skill to select the
best angle or the time of day which will most effectively
display the full beauty of plants.*

My Gardens
in the Mediterranean
by the Vicomte de Noailles

Villa Noailles, a green oasis in the grey olive-clad hills of Grasse

In 1924 I started my first garden at Hyères and I looked for a book which could help a philistine in the Mediterranean Region. By "Mediterranean Region", I understand where the Olive tree constitutes a secular wealth, as well as its fringe zone, where the Orange tree grows well.

I discovered that no book supplied the information I required. Numerous botanical books listed the indigenous or naturalised plants but were only useful to experts already having a knowledge of the gardens on the Riviera. Only the book "Gardening in Sunny Lands" by Mrs. Philip Martineau and by Mrs Edith Wharton, published in English in 1924, proved useful to me. Unfortunately this most valuable book is long out of print and difficult to obtain. This book contained a most useful list of plants suitable for Riviera or Californian gardens. It is this list which I have tried to bring up to date by mentioning a good many plants omitted or which had not reached gardens 50 years ago.

At Hyères, due to the modern architecture of Mallet-Stevens and the location on a slope facing south, without water save as a concession of the town, I first tried succulent plants. Alas, after a few years I discovered that these plants, most of them covered with prickles destined to protect them against the goats, were just as menacing for the hands of human beings. The succulent plants disappeared.

To make a change in height, I had imported from Italy a wagonload of evergreen oaks *(Quercus ilex)*, large saplings. They have grown and at the present time constitute the most happy result of all the plantations, now belonging to the town of Hyères. Under the Almond trees I planted mixed bulbs. Each year, making a note of where it was necessary to modify the colours, I would add bulbs of anemones, tulips, alliums etc. This represented a certain amount of plantation work and a rather large expense, most of the bulbs coming from Van Tubergen in Holland. The result was pleasant for three weeks or a month, coinciding with the blooming of the Almond trees, giving the impression of the flowering meadows in the gothic tapestries.

We departed each year from the South at the end of April or beginning of May to return for Christmas.

During the occupation, I had stayed there for longer periods and had come to the conclusion that with a rationed water concession and a slope burnt by the sun, I would never draw real pleasure from a meridional property.

As soon as I could after the liberation I transported a large number of plants from the garden in Hyères into another garden at Grasse, which, because it was facing West and of course colder, did not permit the culture of Citrus fruits. On the other hand, a large spring at the top of the property supplied 50 cubic meters every 24 hours. A succession of terraces on which grew old Olive trees reached down to a field, bordered by a torrent, pleasant at times but deplorably dry in summer. The farmer was in the habit of grazing his sheep in the field during the dry weather, and on the terraces when the soil was damp. I had planted many Narcisses and other bulbs bellow the trees. This pleased me greatly but had to be given up. Alas, the sheep seemed to appreciate the bulbs even more than I did. They were suppressed. I had also noticed that in a particular spot the grass remained green. I soon became aware that in this zone the Olive trees were unhealthy. The farmer said me : "If you do not drain this new spring, the summer dampness will kill the trees". I thus began to drain all the damp spots on the hillside, with excellent results.

Imprudently I had planted Orange trees on the wide terrace above the field. Very quickly a cold winter made me change my mind.

The previous owner had without success tried a commercial culture of rose trees on the same location. The soil is strong, slightly clayey, sufficiently aired, the poor growth of the rose trees is to me unexplainable.

I must inform the reader that if this information supplied to day is, I believe, approximatively correct, it will not be the same a few years from now.

After the first World war, I and my neighbours, grew Suziana irises, Tuberoses *(Polianthes tuberosa)* and Echiums and I went and admired with envy the Saxatilis Tulips which only really grew well in a garden at Cap Martin.

The second World War brought, and I wonder why? a fatal stroke to the Suziana irises, the most beautiful of all. A few clever gardeners managed to maintain them for ten or twenty years, but they seem to have disappeared in our region, at least for the present.

Fields of Tuberoses *(Polianthes tuberosa)* which bordered the road from Hyères to Toulon lasted longer and one can still, very often, buy cut flowers from the florists on the Riviera, but their cultivation on a large scale seems to have disappeared.

An extremely useful plant though quite common, for which I have much sympathy is *Viburnum tinus,* the Laurustinus, which continues to grow perfectly well but in certain gardens the leaves become yellow without any explanation. Such bushes should be cut down to within a foot of the ground when the new

Carpobrotus edulis, forming extensive carpets above the sea

shoots will produce healthy leaves and for a year or two all will be well but then it will be necessary to start again.

I also remember the times when, during the month of June, there were superb tufts of Madonna lilies *(Lilium candidum)* in front of all the houses of the gate-keepers at level crossings. I do not particularly miss the level crossings but I greatly miss the times when the lilies flowered so easily.

A SHORT HISTORY
OF MEDITERRANEAN GARDENS

Lord Brougham, in 1824, travelling with his ailing daughter to Italy, was held up in Antibes by an epidemic of cholera. Turning back, he chose a seemingly priviliged area, rising above the bay of Cannes and sheltered by the hill on which stood the town. There he built a house and the first British garden was created. Others followed suit, some French, and under the Second Empire, the Vigier garden on the East side of the port of Nice, of which there is no longer any trace, contained a collection of palm trees and imported plants. It seems that many of the plants which we now import were already being used at that time.

A writer, a pamphleteer, but nevertheless a gardener, Alphonse Karr, was the first who thought of sending flowers to the Paris markets, profiting by the newly created railway line. This was the beginning of what has become an important industry.

When in 1860 the area of Nice joined with France, several beautiful gardens were established near Nice, inspired by the gardens of Italy. Hardly a trace of them remains, not even the Arson garden in which in 1914 some terraces were still carried on walls ornamented with shells, and coloured pebbles.

About the beginning of the Second Empire, a member of the Protestant Community Group, M. Gustave Thuret, who suffered from rheumatism, moved to the Antibes peninsula. He was a botanist, interested mainly in seaweeds but he did plant a garden of considerable interest. After his death, his sister-in-law gave the property to the French Government, who built an agricultural research station there.

Then, unexpectedly, during, and particularly after, the First World War, the problem of dust was solved by the introduction of tarmacadam. Also abolished were ladies' corsets! From this it was only a short step to the advent of sunbathing and bathing costumes. People discovered the pleasant resorts of the Côte d'Azur. In Juan-les-Pins, the local policeman walked up and down the beach making sure that both shoulder straps of the mens bathing suits were in order. This was only a few seasons before the vogue of the bikini.

Hotels and villas sprang up like mushrooms all along the coast, but only very few people were interested in summer flowers. No blooms were to be seen in the month of August either on the Croisette, or the Promenade des Anglais!

It was understood that no flowers grew in the summer, and the flower beds waited, empty, for the Autumn Cinerarias.

M. et Mme Pierre Champin at the Chèvre d'Or, profiting by the advice of M. Basil Leng, the most knowledgeable gardener on the Coast, created the first garden to be considered interesting outside of the winter months. Since then many have imitated them.

Gardening
in the Mediterranean
by Roy Lancaster

THE MEDITERRANEAN CLIMATE

In its simplest terms a Mediterranean climate is one of hot and dry summers and cool and moist winters. This in part explains why, in these regions, most plants are active, i.e. growing and flowering during winter than in summer when the sun bakes the soil and causes growth to slow or cease altogether. This does not mean to say of course that the Mediterranean Region as a whole enjoys exactly the same climate. Local variations are plentiful and are controlled by such factors as air circulation, proximity of sea and moutains, etc.

In the Mediterranean Region rainfall mostly occurs between October and April and this is the period when planting should be carried out. Attention to irrigation and watering during the following summer is an important, if not critical, factor in the establishing of newly planted material.

Those gardens where water is available in the form of a spring, well or stream are fortunate indeed and enables their owners to attempt a much wider variety of plants than those gardens without natural water. Fortunately, such is the diversity of plants grown in Mediterranean areas that even those who garden on the rockiest soils in the hottest and driest situations still have a plentiful selection from which to create a successful and satisfying landscape.

Three important characteristics of the natural vegetation of the Mediterranean Region are -
1. the preponderance of evergreen trees and shrubs · over deciduous kinds.
2. the abundance and variety of annual plants.
3. the large variety of bulbous plants.
All three groups are ideally adapted to the extremes of climate and may be intelligently used in the garden scheme. In fact, it is surprising how few gardens in the Mediterranean Region make use of the native trees and shrubs of the surrounding maquis or garrigue. This is even more surprising when one considers the popularity of Mediterranean native plants among gardeners in colder more northerly regions of Europe. It is even possible to find some Mediterranean gardens where every plant is an exotic from another land, a sad reflection on the owner's sympathy with his surroundings.

Most satisfying are those gardens where foreign exotics rub shoulders with the native vegetation. Where *Cistus* and rosemary, lavender and thyme find company with *Acacia, Ceanothus, Datura* and *Yucca.*

It is not generally realised by gardeners that other areas of the world enjoy a Mediterranean climate. Apart from the Mediterranean Region itself, (see charte page 10), four other areas experience conditions which are very similar to those of the Mediterranean Sea Basin. These are found in California, central Chile, the Cape Region of South Africa and south-western and southern Australia. It has been estimated that approximately 25,000 species of flowering plants occur wild in these five areas, and well over half are found nowhere else. This incredible number of plants represents an immense paintbox from which the gardener may choose whichever colours best suit his ideas and imagination.

An interesting fact relating to the climate of these five regions concerns the difference in seasons between the northern and southern hemispheres. The summers of the Mediterranean Region and California (May to October) are the winters of Chile, South Africa and Australia, and this difference often shows most markedly when plants from one hemisphere are cultivated in the other.

GROWING TENDER PLANTS IN OTHER REGIONS.

Finally, lest it be thought that only in regions of the world enjoying a Mediterranean climate can such plants be grown, it should be pointed out that tender plants or those of borderline hardiness are also possible in countries with a colder climate. The factors which make this possible are numerous and diverse but include the presence of favourable but localised winter condidtions as well as the provision of artificial shelter.

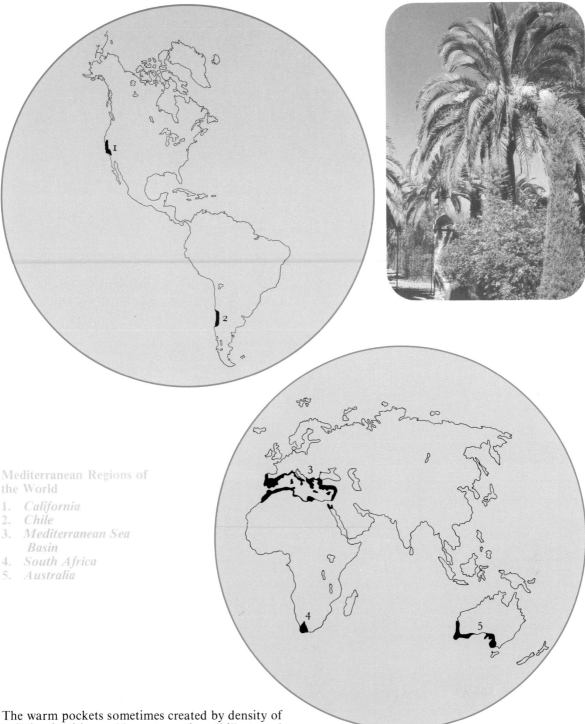

The warm pockets sometimes created by density of building in cities and large towns is well illustrated in London where a wide range of tender plants may be found flourishing in sheltered gardens and courtyards.

The south and south-western regions of the British Isles as well as south-west Europe, southern United States, southern Japan and North Island of New Zealand provide conditions conducive to the cultivation of Mediterranean plants.

With luck and determination (two important elements in successful gardening) tender plants may be grown outside in the most surprising places and whilst frost may make their benefits short-lived this should in no way deter the gardener from taking a chance. Nothing ventured nothing gained should be his motto.

THE MEDITERRANEAN YEAR

Autumn rains lasting for long periods (falling especially at night) bring to an end the drought and dust of summer and start most plants into growth. This is a soft and gentle season with many late flowers and fruits. It slowly gives way to winter which brings nights and days of contrasting temperatures due to the relative absence of clouds and fog. At the end of January winds from the continent blow cold and bring snow to high ground. However, frost and extreme cold rarely occur, in fact as far apart as 1709, 1820 and 1956, when pines and olives were badly damaged.

Spring arrives between March and April, when the majority of flowers open and plants both in gardens and in the wild join in a mad rush to attract and impress. This is the mildest and most colourful time of the year for gardeners and visitors alike.

Summer arrives suddenly, almost without warning, and the long hot, dry days are relieved only by the contrasting coolness and freshness of the nights. Plant life both outside and inside the garden slows down or assumes a state of suspended animation (like a hedgehog hibernating for the winter).

Average temperatures for *January* and *July* respectively are -

Perpignan	$7^0 7$	$23^0 8$
Montpellier	$5^0 8$	$22^0 3$
Avignon	$5^0 3$	$23^0 3$
Marseille	$7^0 0$	$22^0 8$
Nice	$8^0 3$	$22^0 4$

Rainfall for three representative locations -

	Summer	Winter
Marseille	76 mm.	164 mm.
Montpellier	93 mm.	176 mm.
Nice	82 mm.	236 mm.

Mediterranean Sea Basin

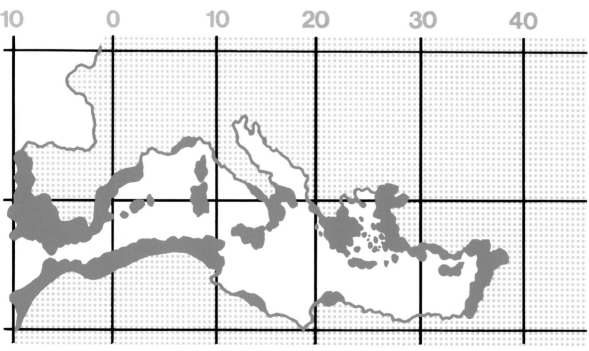

A short guide to planting

GARDEN PLANNING :

In medium size gardens, the basic layout is created with hedges, of various heights, often hard pruned.

Hedges from	10 cm to	1.5 m :	various boxes (*Buxus*), slow growing
—	50 cm to	1m :	Rosemary (erect varieties)
—	25 cm to	1.5 m :	Myrtle (*Myrtus communis*)
—	1 m to	2.5 m :	*Pittosporum tobira*
—	1 m to	4 m :	Bay (*Laurus nobilis*)
—	1 m to	12 m :	Italian cypress (*Cupressus sempervirens* 'Strica').

A hedge of erect rosemary will be perfect in three years time but will lose its leaves at the base when five years old and will have to be replaced after the tenth. It is perhaps best to double the hedge by a row of box which will take its place later.

Monterey Cypress (*Cupressus macrocarpa*) for hedging grows very rapidly but it is necessary to clip it drastically once a year with the risk of a tree dying now and then. The alternative consists in letting them grow without clipping which presents more security but sacrifices a great deal of space in the garden.

The Italian cypress (*Cupressus sempervirens* 'Stricta') grows rapidly and can hardly be limited in height and after a few years its high dark columns sadden a garden.

PROTECTION AGAINST DOMINATING WINDS :

On flat land, well planned plantations to break the winds provide the chance to improve micro-climates.

For these wind-breaks, it must not be imagined that a wall will solve the problem. A strong wind beats down the air behind the wall creating turbulance at a distance of about two and a half times the wall height. It is preferable to filter the wind through

La Leonina, a rich collection of subtropical vegetation

bushes or trees. In the case of a wall, the trees, particularly if they are evergreens and rise above the wall, filter the wind and are an excellent protection. However, their roots risk impending the plants. In most gardens it is necessary to fall back upon the various cypresses, or even bamboo hedges when the type of garden permits a somewhat exotic appearance.

In the vicinity of the sea, hedges can be made up with *Atriplex halimus, Pistachia lentiscus, Griselinia littoralis, Drymis winteri,* etc.

Plants suffer from the drought even more than the wind. So as to be able to plant creepers against a wall, the owner will have to plant at each angle of the house a plant sufficiently high to ensure protection. 2Laurus nobilis (Bay Laurel , Sweet Bay) is perfect from this point of view. The Italian cypress is less appropriate tending to thin out at the proximity of the angles. *Pittosporum tobira* is suitable but hardly rises above 2.5 m.

CULTIVATION OF THE GARDEN :

A - Nature of the soil (most frequently chalky around the Mediterranean area).

B - Watering : the owner may find himself faced with one of the following situations :

1. A permanent spring of water is available or a well with a more or less constant water level.

2. A sufficient water concession is available and at a reasonable price.

3. There is neither spring nor concession.

In the first instance, an electric pump will supply the necessary pressure and cause hardly any trouble. But water from a well (or even a municipal canalization) is often cold ; it is therefore useful to use one of the numerous water sprinklers, the tiny drops of which will have gained several degrees of warmth before falling to the ground.

In situation 2, no problem.

In the third instance it is possible to have an interesting garden with plants resisting the drought, such as those with tomentose leaves, succulent plants, etc. In Greece, lawns are made with *Achillea millefolium* mown like grass and the effect is good. *Parkinsonia,* a bush with yellow flowers, blooms all summer without watering and it is the same for *Beschorneria,* etc., in spring.

The best solution for the new gardener in the region is to observe the plants which grow well in the neighbouring gardens and to learn from others successes and failures.

Numerous are the sweet scented bushy or climbing plants. As one walks round a garden along the same paths, there are inevitably spots to which one goes to more frequently than others, but as the scent from the flowers does not give pleasure for more than a few seconds, it is advisable to group a choice of scented plants in various strategic positions. Here broadly is the succession of the flowering season starting from December :

Sarcococca - various species
Chimonanthus praecox
Daphne odora
Viburnum carlesii and hybrids
Viburnum bitchiuense
Viburnum x juddii
Coronilla glauca
Clematis armandii
Stauntonia species
Pittosporum species
Jasminum polyanthum
Osmanthus fragrans 'Aurantiaca'
Osmanthus x fortunei
Osmanthus heterophyllus
Buddleia officinalis
Buddleia auriculata

The beginner creating a Mediterranean garden likes to use the plants he already knows. However, he must expect for disappointments. Many plants coming from other regions will only give mediocre results, for example, delphinium, *Digitalis,* lupins, *Phlox,* herbaceous paeonies, *Delphinium,* etc.

However, a large number of bulbs and rhizomes suitable in northern regions will perfectly succeed these include *Amaryllis, Nerine,* etc.

Some beginners will be tempted to grow plants disliking chalk, *Rhododendron, Azalea, Camellia,* etc., but these schould only be planted in acid soils or in pots.

The soils in the Esterel, for example which are suitable for the commercial cultivation of Mimosa (*Acacia*), are also suitable for camellias, azaleas and rhododendrons. Elsewhere, it is necessary to spread acid soil 60 cm. deep above the local chalky soil which should then normally permit their culture.

It will be more difficult to battle against the sun and the dryness of the air in summer. The sun is particularly dangerous in case of reflection of walls facing south or west. This applies only to gardens in Mediterranean regions.

Watering can also cause problems for calcifuge plants, the water in these regions often being chalky.

C. Noailles.

Some Mediterranean Gardens

by Roy Lancaster.

Hillside near Grasse
with "Cypress Sentinels"

A riotous assembly
of olives, palms and cypresses

SOME MEDITERRANEAN GARDENS

Most visitors see the Mediterranean gardens in the spring when they are undoutedly at their best (mainly because they are planted with this season in mind), but other seasons bring their own colours and delights and as my first introduction to these gardens was in the autumn I shall describe my thoughts and reactions at that time.

Driving down the Autoroute, a long way south of Lyon, the Mediterranean Region rushed to greet us in a great waft of heat and brightness. Gradually, as the kilometres raced away, the terrain began to change and soon olives and almonds replaced apples and pears as the dominant orchards. The grey of the olives speaking more than anything else of the Mediterranean Region, their grey leaves on crooked boughs like so many crouching figures, lined hills and hot arid valleys. In late winter and spring these same regions are pink with myriad almond and peach blossoms.

Our entry into the Mediterranean Region was complete with the arrival of stone pines (*Pinus pinea*), their parasoled heads congregated on low sun blasted hills and scattered in every direction even approaching the Autoroute. Low roadside vegetation and scrub reflected the same southern warmth, as *Juniperus oxycedrus, Pistacia teribinthus, Cistus albidus* and *C. monspeliensis,*

Pines by a road in Provence

rosemary, lavender, thyme and countless others combined to fill the air with their rich and varied aromas.

Turning north from Cannes we passed hillsides overflowing with mimosa (*Acacia dealbata* and *A. decurrens*) which in winter fill the valleys with sun as their feathered branches burst into a riot of yellow.

Our centre for the following week was to be Grasse sitting in perfumed isolation on a sun-facing hillside. Here lay our first call : the Villa Noailles, home of the Vicomte de Noailles.

VILLA NOAILLES - GRASSE

The morning was well advanced as we walked in the blistering heat along the main drive, the sun burning its way into our brains, the olive trees in the pasture below a grey haze of heat and oil. Passing through an imposing stone entrance we found ourselves immediately entering another world : a world of dark and cool, a cobbled yard where shadows prevailed and the light sneaked in wherever the canopy allowed. Here an old flat-topped, wide-spreading, lime tree dominated, filling the yard, its boughs occasionally supported on crutches of wood. Here also, beneath the lime's sheltering boughs, stood camellias in large clay tubs, whilst other evergreens - periwinkles, ivies, *Sarcococca* and box added variety to the scene. A recess in a nearby stone wall contained a spring, the water tumbling from tier to tier amidst shrouding maindenhair fern (*Adiantum* sp.). The sound of water carried us through a partition to observe a stream of cool liquid plunging from a stone channel into a misty pool in which giant carp silently moved.

The whole area was self-contained with a soothing admixture of steps, stones, cobbles and tiles, affording varying levels of satisfaction and appreciation.

The shadowy court though, was merely a preliminary through which we passed into a garden belonging to the world of children's fairy stories. An enchanted garden where cool shade and the constant refreshing sound of water beguiled the visitor into forgetting the recent sun-bleached hillsides outside.

We followed a paved walk alongside a high wall where a double row of flared pipes emptied water into elongated troughs. The whole wall-face was softened by the misty green fronds of maiden hair fern as well as polypody (*Polypodium*) and harts tongue fern *(Phyllitis),* whilst *Helxine* chequered the darkest corners with its green film. The sound as one passed was a symphony of cool suggestion, refreshing to parched throats and dulled minds.

Potted evergreens in the courtyard at Villa Noailles

We continued through a series of terraces, some shaded others sunlit, flanked by borders, in which both hardy and delicate plants occurred in happy array. A 4m. specimen of the Brazilian Coral Tree - *Erythrina crista-galli,* its long sprays of brilliant red flowers thrusting out from trifoliate leaves, was faced across a grass walk by *Abelia* x *grandiflora,* one of the longest flowering and most satisfactory of all hardy shrubs. Nearby towered the dark evergreen mass of the tough and hightly utilitarian *Cotoneaster lacteus. Coronilla glauca* jostled with *Garrya elliptica,* and clumps of *Myrtus communis tarentina* grew strongly with *Sycopsis sinensis* and *Acer oblongum.*

One long walk lay beneath sapling *Quercus ilex,* their tall, slender, grey stems crowding the path, their feet bathed by pink and white *Cyclamen hederifolium* and occasional leafy patches of *Iris japonica.*

Soon we reached an area of grassy terraces dotted with pollarded olives. From here we could see the sun-drenched hillsides and their red-roofed dwellings guarded by cypress sentinels.

Just as the heat again began to make itself felt a small lily-pool beckoned and we were led into an enclosed seated refuge formed of bays (*Laurus nobilis*) trained on a wire and metal cage. From here one could sit and watch the azure and copper spangled dragonflies darting across the lily pads, whilst somewhere behind and below a cacophony of sound betrayed a waterfall. So cool and detached was this place that even the urgent cries of a buzzard from the hot crags above seemed of another world.

Jasminum angulare clambered along a wall, its white tubular flowers offering a rich fragrance to the air competing with the evergreen *Osmanthus fragans* 'Aurantiacus', whose tiny, richly scented flowers are an unusual shade of orange, like that of chanterelles.

Lespedeza thunbergii was planted on banks and other raised places where its long, purple flowered, stems tumbled in graceful waves into still waters or into the path at one's feet.

A great tuft of channelled, narrow, grey-green leaves belonged to *Hesperaloe englemanii,* a native of Texas and a lover of sunny dry places. From among the leaves appeared a stem 2m. high bearing at its extremity a lax raceme of creamy-yellow, red flushed flowers, tubular in bud.

We were surprised here to find an aviary full of colourful screeching budgerigars, but it wasn't the birds so much as the aviary which caught our attention. In the face of its end wall was set a charming Delft tableau which in its turn was framed by the closely clipped growth of the New Zealand *Muehlenbeckia complexa,* a brilliant use for an otherwise wild and uncontrollable vine.

A large meadow at the bottom of the slope by the river contained a mixture of trees including various Japanese cherries and several named cultivars of *Magnolia* x *soulangiana* which flaunt purple and white goblets on naked twigs in spring.

In the bottom corner of the garden stood a magnificent example of the Dawn Redwood - *Metasequoia glyptostroboides* - which measured at least 20m. tall with a buttressed lower trunk.

Our ascent through the terraces took in several peat-filled borders in which grew some good examples of the lime-hating *Corylopsis ; Halesia ; Sassafras* and *Michelia fuscata.* Then we were passing a wide parasoled *Cupressus lusitanica* with intense blue-grey plumose branches flanked by dark hedges. Eventually we found ourselves back in the sunshine on the drive, the magic of the morning locked in the villa and in our minds.

LA CHÈVRE D'OR - BIOT

La Chèvre d'Or the garden of Monsieur and Madame Champin rests in the hills behind Nice facing the picturesque village of Biot. A small but intimate cobbled and tiled courtyard connects the house with the garden. We came early in the evening and the rare scent of *Cestrum nocturnum* greeted our arrival and cast a fragrant spell over the surrounding terraces.

Ceanothus and *Genista monosperma* at Chèvre d'Or

Orange trees and box partitions at Chèvre d'Or

Dwarf pomegranates, *Punica granatum* 'Pumila' made neat bushes in several tubs and pots, and already their small multi-seeded fruits were beginning to swell.

Draping a low wall with its tendrilled stems was *Ampelopsis brevipedunculata* 'Elegans', a charming ornamental vine with white marbled leaves and clusters of tiny grapes exhibiting several colours at once. *Plumbago capensis* had been trained into almond trees and its slender stems tumbled from the branches in showers of pale sky blue.

A small orchard appeared, trees in naked soil. The dark bareness however was relieved by groups of tall white foxtails, snow-pokers thrusting up like rockets from giant bulbs. This was *Urginea maritima* a native of Mediterranean shores and a lover of sun and drought. In winter handsome strap-shaped leaves appear.

On a higher terrace we were confronted by a young but impressive palm - *Erythea armata* - with large, glaucous, fan-shaped leaves on thorny stems. Walls were clothed with vines and creepers amongst which the white flowered *Mandevilla suaveolens* was finished and hung with slender pods, whilst *Tecoma ricalosiana* still flaunted its clusters of blush-pink tubular flowers striped darker in the throat.

All too soon evening drew its curtains of darkness and the terraces filled with shadows as cleverly hidden lights suddenly appeared to change completely the daytime emphasis.

LA GAROUPE - CAP D'ANTIBES

Completely different is the garden of Mr. and Mrs. Anthony Norman at La Garoupe on the Cap d'Antibes.

La Garoupe, *Beschorneria yuccoides* beneath *Pinus halepensis*

The gull-white house sits on high ground over-looking the Mediterranean. A series of broad shallow steps leads the eye in a long arrow-straight line to where the sea glitters like a million diamonds. We arrived in the morning sun, its heat lying like a blanket on the garden, silencing birds and beasts. Here the overall landscape effect is considered more important than the multiplicity of plants.

The garden on the south side of the house is reserved for sun-loving summer subjects, whilst the comparatively cooler areas to the north of the house are planted almost entirely for spring effect.

We began our walk on the south side, leaving the wide patio flanked by the night-scented *Cestrum nocturnum,* then descended a broad flight of steps. The balustrades here were ablaze with the orange-flame flower clusters of *Tecomaria capensis* which scrambled urgently over stone and space crowding its stems with glossy, small divided leaves.

A large parterre presented itself, a vast low design of grey lavender and rosemary ; grey and green lavender cotton (*Santolina*) and green box. Carefully clipped twice yearly, the whole layout refurbished every seven or eight years. The formality continued in a series of small self-contained gardens, one planted with pansies and stocks for spring effect and then replaced with blue and white petunias to continue until autumn. At the time of our visit red and pink *Impatiens* were herded into small beds edged with *Santolina neapolitana* and featuring specimen standard tangerine trees.

A white garden next appeared, a circle of orange trees under-planted with *Euonymus japonicus* 'Macrophyllus Albus' and white hydrangeas. The centre of this garden was occupied by a small hexagonal pool in which floated cream waterlilies and the brown spangled heads of *Cyperus alternifolius* borne on three-angled stems.

We next found ourselves in a large enclosed area occupied by a swimming pool, at one end of which was an open fronted pergola supporting a pink *Tecoma,* together with *Thunbergia grandiflora* hanging its clusters of magnificent lilac-blue, white throated flowers. Here also a splendid double pink *Hibiscus rosa-sinensis* flourished alongside the more familiar single scarlet form.

Returning to the parterre we passed several huge clumps of a lovely pink-plumed pampas grass (*Cortaderia selloana* 'Rosea') and tall branched specimens of *Yucca guatemalensis* with its handsome leaf ruffs and panicles of white flowers.

Next we descended the central path which connects the house with the sea. On either side lay areas of dry rock-strewn soil where fine groupings of *Yucca gloriosa* stood, for all the world like ranks of armoured soldiers bristling with lances and holding aloft banners of ivory white. Huge grey specimens

Where the maquis meets the sea at La Garoupe

of *Agave americana* were planted at intervals, whilst between these forests of rigid leaves the apple blossom pink umbels of *Amaryllis belladonna* were just fading, having flooded the ground with their delicate colour during previous weeks.

Now other plants made colourful contributions to the scene especially the multicoloured *Lantana camara* and beds of *Clarkia* and *Petunia.* Sentinel-like cypresses flanked the path and two round-headed *Acacia decurrens* were already crowded with flower buds ready for the coming winter.

The main path stopped above the water and we gazed across a small rock encircled bay to where the Mediterranean sea marked a long horizon of aquamarine. Below us the rocks repelled the sun's blast and succulents ran down in waves and rivulets led by the robust Hottentot Fig (*Carpobrotus edulis.*)

Colourful bands of *Iris germanica* and *Cyclamen persicum* at La Garoupe

On all sides the maquis thrived, huge areas of wild low scrub in which *Cistus monspeliensis* and *C. albidus* predominated. *Myrtus communis; Phillyrea angustifolia; Coronilla glauca; Cneorum tricocum; Calycotome infesta* and *Lavandula stoechas* also contribute colour and aroma to this dense native tangle which is allowed to run up to and occasionally into the garden. There exists here a splendid balance of the native and the exotic, a mixed community where all individuals have a place and a contribution to make.

Tall and often crooked specimens of the Aleppo Pine (*Pinus halepensis*) waved like dancers above the sea and overshadowed parts of the maquis giving welcome cover and protecting the majority of the garden from salt spray.

In spring much of the southern area of the garden is alive with fragrant freesias and paper-white narcissi which have been allowed to spread unchecked between and beneath planted shrubs and trees.

The garden on the north side of the house lies on a gentle slope and consists mainly of orchards. Here is a winter garden lined with old olive trees and flanked by huge drifts of *Cyclamen persicum* which provide broad bands of colour in the spring. Later the task is taken over by Flag iris which are again planted in flanking drifts and produce a wide range of both rich and pastel shades to the scene.

An orange orchard is underplanted with floribunda roses and surrounded by small flowering trees such as crabs (*Malus*) and cherries (*Prunus*). Among the best of the latter are 'Shimidsu Sakura', 'Shirofugen' and 'Shirotae', all with spreading heads and predominantly white blossoms. Spiraeas of several species are commonly planted here as also is *Exochorda*, the bridal wreath, mainly for their white flowers in spring.

The garden at La Garoupe is a triumph of design over disorder. Each path has been carefully considered, each vista confirmed or reclaimed. Variety of plants there certainly is but they are made to "pay for their keep" and the results are dramatic proof of the wisdom of patience over impetuosity.

VILLA VAL RAHMEH
MENTON - GARAVAN

On a hillside above Menton-Garavan lies the villa "Val Rahmeh", former home and garden of Miss Campbell and now the Jardin Botanique Exotique. It is situated in the Avenue St. Jaques and is open to the public on most days.

We entered the garden one morning and made our way up a short drive lined on one side by the palm *Phoenix canariensis*, whose impressive heads are such a feature of Mediterranean promenades.

The clay-coloured walls of the villa are clothed with a wide variety of vines and creepers including a large *Phaedranthus buccinatorius*, its flowers just opening, long tubes of pale orange with a rose-coloured mouth. *Quamoclit coccinea* was also here, its small, deeply lobed leaves ideal foil for the equally small but glowing red flowers.

On the lawns at the south of the villa grew several beautiful plants maintained as isolated specimens. Most beautiful of all were several *Datura* species - Angel's trumpets - of which *D. cornigera* 'Knightii' with double white flowers, *D. candida* 'Rosea' with rose-flushed cream coloured flowers, and *D. versicolor* with cream flowers flushed apricot were the most outstanding.

A widespreading bush of *Solanum rantonnettii* only 1.5m. high possessed densely leafy stems arching beneath the weight of multitudes of pale purple flowers each with a yellow staminal beak.

At one end of the lawn stood a specimen of the Pepper tree - *Schinus molle* - from South America. This is a small tree of delicate appearance with its gracefully pendant branches and deeply divided fern-like leaves. It is commonly planted in the Mediterranean Region, thriving in the heat.

A balustrade and a pergola at the far end of the lawn supported several unusual climbers including the handsome *Thunbergia grandiflora* and *Solanum wendlandii* the latter with racemes of lavender-blue flowers 4 cm. across. From this point we gazed down into a lower garden where orange and grapefruit trees flourished.

In the sunken garden a large selection of interesting and often attractive plants grew. *Debregeasia edulis*, a large shrub with silver backed leaves; *Acacia vestita* producing fountains of slender, downy, grey branches; *Duranta plumieri* the pigeon berry with small bright yellow berries replacing the pale lilac flowers; *Persea americana*, the Avocado Pear, up to 10 m. high and a large fruiting specimen of the twining *Actinidia chinensis* or Cape Gooseberry.

Having descended into the sunken garden we found ourselves continually stopping as new and exciting plants appeared. These included *Quillaia saponaria* the Soap-bark tree of Chile; *Tetrapanax papyriferum* with its huge deeply lobed leaves quite the handsomest foliage plant I had seen for some time.
Arundinaria longifolia from Mexico with extremely narrow leaves produced in dense bunches caught my attention, whilst at the other extreme was *Bambusa macroculmis* producing stout canes up to 13 m tall.

In a nearby pond lived the Egyptian papyrus - *Cyperus papyrus* - an attractive plant with 2-3 m. jade-green triangular stems supporting large spherical heads of coffee-coloured spikelets.

From the bottom of this garden superb views up the valley were possible and one's gaze reached to the limestone ridge and crags, brilliant white in the sun. We followed a path which led along the foot of a wall where climbers clung. At our feet lay the fallen flowers of *Thunbergia* for all the world like delicate fragments of blue sky.

A set of iron steps led us out of the lower garden into a small grassy area in the centre of which a pool with the inevitable waterlilies and lotus (*Nelumbo*) attracted a host of gleaming dragonflies. From here we gained a clear view of the villa above and we could better appreciate the huge piles of *Bougainvillea*, *Thunbergia* and *Tecoma* against the big supporting wall. Above all rose a wide maquis-clad, sun-bleached panorama in which Aleppo pines appeared as green stains.

Again we were reminded of the skill shown by those early Mediterranean garden makers in bringing outside landscapes and individual features into the confines of the garden.

In the pool garden several plants demanded attention and a huge pink flowered *Hibiscus moscheutus* hybrid was one of them. Nearby grew the purple flushed form of the Castor-oil plant - *Ricinus communis* - exhibiting striking crimson fruiting spikes, whilst *Brunfelsia calycina* changed its flowers from purple to white, both colours being apparent on the one plant. One of my favourite plants, the Lion's-ear - *Leonitis leonurus* - here reached 2 m., its square stems bearing pairs of long narrow leaves and axillary whorls of strange downy orange flowers.

Senecio grandifolius, true to its name, carried large boldly toothed leaves, and *Dahlia arborea,* also from Mexico, had developed a 3 m. clump of stout leafy stems but with no sign of its brilliant red flowers.

After a final look at its botanical treasures we reluctantly left the villa Val Rahmeh by way of a cool shaded corner where ferns luxuriated and pads continued by Mr. Cecil Hanbury, the garden is now in the care of the Italian government.

Although the present garden has declined since the halcyon years it nevertheless remains set in a superb position on a hillside above the sea and still retains some of the magic and poetry endowed upon it by its makers.

Villa Val Rahmeh, its pool and creeper clad walls

of *Streptocarpus* x *kewensis* flaunted purple-blue tubular flowers on long stems.

LA MORTOLA - VENTIMIGLIA

A garden I had long known about from books, articles and various personal accounts was the famous spectacle at *La Mortola* just across the Italian border near Ventimiglia. Built by Sir Thomas Hanbury towards the end of the last century and

We entered the garden from the cliff top walk and made our way along a path which soon crossed the Via Aurelia, an ancient Roman road. The first plant to surprise us here was a giant *Acanthus montanus* of 6 m. with woody based stems and long spine-toothed, deeply cut leaves.

Sorbus domestica, the Service tree, was heavy with fruits the size of crab apples and of a pale green with russet cheeks. Those which had fallen were purple-brown and ready to eat and we quickly filled our mouths with the sweet rotting pulp. The silvery-downy leaves of *Acacia* x *hanburyana* caught our attention as we climbed up the steep path that searches the western flank of the garden. Here in a shallow ravine was a lost world of shade and wild tangled undergrowth where fig, *Robinia,* bay, oak, *Eucalyptus* and pine fought for the light.

(*Tilia*) and is famous for the lightness of its wood, lighter even than cork.

Eventually we attained the upper terrace path and immediately gained superb views of the lower garden and the sea beyond. A large colony of the banana (*Musa sapientium*) grew on a bank by the path, and several stems bore heavy hands of fruit. Very similar in stature and leaf is the closely related

A terrace at La Mortola, flanked by Cycas and Yucca guatemalensis on the left and Encephalartos, Erythea and Cypress on the right.

Other trees on the slope were neglected or mal-treated, a sad reflection of present times. One tree *Cheirostemon platanoides* from Guatemala had leaves like a plane (*Platanus*) and reached 15 m. high, whilst the orange fruited *Pittosporum undulatum* was 8 m. *Senecio petasites* was a loose-habited shrub up to 2 m. with large rounded scalloped and felted leaves. Even the rare *Entelea arborescens* from New Zealand flourished here. This shrub belongs to the same family as the linden

Stretlitzea alba which grew nearby, both very effective foliage plants for sheltered sites where strong winds cannot shred their leaves. From this high altar of the garden we gazed down through plantations of exotic trees onto banks of succulents and plants of spiky nature. One area contained a mixed collection of fine palms in which *Erythea; Phoenix; Trachycarpus* and *Washingtonia* domi-nated. Tragically several of the most lofty specimens had been damaged by vandals.

A steep bank contained a wide collection of plants with rosetted leaves. Here the monster blue clumps of *Agave franzosinii* were particularly outstanding, whilst *Puya spathacea; Dasylirion serratifolium; Aloe mitriformis* and *Yucca guatemalensis* offered support. The whole collection presented a picture of hostility with ranks and rings of lances, spears and serrated swords. From this place we looked down a long vista of steps and flanking cypress trees to where a fountain played in a small pool surrounded by flame and yellow cannas.

Our path now led between large imposing crowds of *Cycas revoluta* and *Encephalartus altensteinii* and on to where a low gnarled tree of *Acacia abyssinica* displayed clusters of green ferny leaves and spherical heads of white stamens. Paths led and crossed, converged and diverged with bewildering irregularity, and at times we wondered if we were not in some vast maze where, instead of walls or hedges, new scenes, flowers, fountains and vistas appeared to bewitch the eye and confuse the mind.

An orchard of apples and pears contained several trees which demanded attention, trees such as *Koelreuteria integrifolia,* a most effective specimen of 12 m. with a large spreading head of branches bearing bold deeply divided leaves and huge terminal panicles of yellow flowers. Nearby an old tree of the Persimmon (*Diospyros kaki*) was shedding its large tomato-like fruits full of sweet pulp. Around this area an old wooden pergola supported several attractive climbing plants including *Passiflora mixta* with pendulous pink flowers. The most spectacular plant here however was *Datura versicolor,* a large specimen which leant against the wooden framework and hung its pink flushed, long tapered trumpets in showers above one's head.

We had reached the lower reaches of the garden and a flight of narrow steps led us down to the beach where lay the debris of a thousand tides. The sun had completed its daily tour and now only vestiges of its presence remained as gilded clouds and trappings in the western sky. We made our way along the rock-strewn shore and up the cliff path. Before regaining the car we turned for one last look at La Mortola now sliding into evening's grasp. The trees appeared as black shapes huddled to the hillside. We imagined we could smell the jasmine there and the resin in the pines, but it must have been a dream. Like a dream La Mortola lingers in the memory, its paths, pools, steps and stones part of paradise, its flowers and trees of another world.

VILLA ROQUEBRUNE

No commentary on Mediterranean Gardens could be considered complete without mention of the Villa Roquebrune, home of Mrs. N. Warre. Here is a splendid example of a garden won from a reluctant and uncompromising terrain. It is situated on the south-west shoulder of Cap Martin, descending in a series of terraces towards the sea. Begun in 1902 by Mrs. Warre and her first husband, Mr. E. Bainbridge, the garden was literally scratched from the rock, and walls were constructed to accomodate imported soil. The story of the Villa Roquebrune is one of patience and determination, and although age and the elements now take their toll, the pattern set by its makers is as strong today as in the beginning.

The garden is a treasury of plants, an Aladdin's cave of rare and elusive gems. From the very first, beautiful plants appear and the wall just inside the main entrance supports a fair introductory selection with *Jasminum mesneyi* and the sweet-scented *J. polyanthum* fighting it out with the striking canary-yellow trumpets of *Bignonia unguis-cati.* Here also lean the long stems of *Buddleia madagascariensis* whose long sprays of yellow flowers during winter ideally compliment the grey leaves. Walls, rails and banks throughout the garden are dressed with choice climbers, of which *Rosa 'La Follette'; R. laevigata, Solandra maxima, Phaedranthus buccinatorius, Bignonia australis, Kennedia comptoniana, Clematis armandii* and *Mandevilla suaveolens* are but a few.

There are several different mimosas which explode into golden blossom in winter. *Acacia* x *hanburyana* is one such with handsome silver-grey foliage, whilst for elegance of habit, little can match the charming pendulous sprays of *A. 'Clair de Lune',* an outstanding member of a highly ornamental group.

Blue is a colour often missing or sparse in gardens, but at Villa Roquebrune it is well represented. The mass plantings of the pale blue-flowered *Hebe hulkeana* and the grey leaved *Teucrium fruticans* are heightened during winter by the deep blue of *Lithospermum rosmarinifolium.*

Covering a slope above the drive is one of the finest examples of the Purple Wreath - *Petrea volubilis* - to be seen outside of its native Mexico. Its sprays of deep violet-mauve contrast effectively with the pink lanterns of *Passiflora antioquiensis* from Colombia. Among the many cacti and succulent plants, perhaps the most extraordinary when in flower is *Agave attenuata,* the swan-neck agave, whose tall spectacular greenish-yellow spikes curve downwards in growing old.

There are many rare and attractive trees which flourish and somehow manage to find enough substenance in the rock bed. The June flowering lilac-blossomed *Jacaranda mimosifolia* occurs in several places, whilst two of the most graceful conifers are present in the shape of *Cupressus cashmeriana* and *C. lusitanica* 'Glauca Pendula', both with grey-blue drooping sprays. The Australian

A glorious assortment of plants at the Villa Roquebrune

silk oak - *Grevillea robusta* - is represented by a substantial tree, whilst from South Africa comes *Calodendrum capense,* the Cape chestnut, with its large loose clusters of maroon freckled, pinky-mauve flowers.

Around the house one comes across piles of colourful pelargoniums tumbling from rocks and pots, and nearby large clumps of erect paddle-shaped leaves release the striking crane-like flowers of the bird-of-paradise - *Strelitzia reginae.*

One of the most striking shrubs in Spring is *Genista monosperma* with its clouds of milk-white pea flowers. Less striking but equally desirable is the rare *Calliandra tweedyi,* a slender-stemmed shrub with prettily divided leaves and rounded clusters of scarlet-stamened flowers in Spring.

The white trumpeted *Beaumontia grandiflora* holds the attention in May with its powerful sweet perfume, whilst in early spring appear the unusual mahogany-red spikes of the Australian *Templetonia retusa.*

As in many other Mediterranean gardens Villa Roquebrune is coloured in season with the massed flowers of bulbous plants and carpeting annuals and perennials, freesias, *Amaryllis, Arctotis,* mesembryanthemums, tulips and callandrinias all take their place on the floral stage and help to make this absorbing garden a small but unforgettable part of Riviera history.

This short review of a handful of Riviera gardens is necessarily a personal one. A hundred people could write accounts of these same gardens and each would be different, but then, surely this is the mark of a successful garden in that it presents different facets, scenes and ideas that change with the time of the day each day of the year ?

Some gardens may take one's breath away with the splendour of the view and vistas to be had from their lofty terraces. Others amaze with the style or dominance of their architecture, whilst some present collections of plants sumptuous to behold and bewildering in their variety and form.

Few gardens combine all the above facets and those that do are monuments to the past rather than pointers to the future. Such gardens are an important part of history and must be spared the planners pen and the auctioneers shattering blows. Gardens like the Villa "Val Rahmeh" are examples of how past glories can be maintained to an acceptable standard. The private gardens of the future, however, must perforce be smaller and, with limitations in space,new concepts and combinations must be found. Some such gardens already exist and many others will doubtless follow.

The Mediterranean garden is a continuing feature, a garden for all seasons and although its size and layout may be drastically changed, its flowers will live on, presenting the same cosmopolitan face to the world.

> Gardens of the sun.
> Where colours, scents
> And subtle shifts of harmony
> Are one long horizon.

La Garoupe
Chrysanthemum frutescens with *Datura sanguinea* in background

Echium gathered round a fallen pine at La Garoupe

Pictorial dictionary of plants for Mediterranean Gardens

The Mediterranean Region, especially the Riviera, is famous for the
wealth of flowering and foliage plants found in its gardens.
Visitors from colder more northerly regions are
impressed by the exotics which flourish here and provide
such a wonderful contrast to the plants of their own gardens and
parks. Palm lined boulevards and gardens filled with
luxuriant vegetation are just two of the
memories derived from holidays in the Mediterranean, and each year
more and more visitors to these regions wonder
at and photograph her floral treasures.

The following selection of descriptions and photographs is, in part,
a guide to some of the more popular plants
grown in Mediterranean gardens. It is also intended
as a guide for those making new gardens in these regions. In the
following pages will be found many of those
plants without which no Mediterranean garden is complete. We have
also included enough rare and
unusual plants to titillate, we hope, the palate
of more experienced gardeners.

---

*We have given the gardener reference marks for the plants suitable for specific sites. The marks
given below indicate those which can be planted from a point of view of hardiness.
Obviously no two gardens are necessarily the same from a climatical point of view
and a certain amount of experiment may be needed to establish which plants
are the most suitable for one's own site.*

✹ Plants capable of growing without difficulty in gardens in the vicinity of isolated LEMON
trees.

❄ Plants capable of growing in gardens where LEMON trees are only grown against a wall
facing South.

○ Plants capable of growing in gardens where ORANGE trees grow without the protection
of a South facing wall.

✖ Plants capable of growing in gardens where ORANGE trees can only be grown against
a South wall.

✳ Plants capable of growing in gardens where CITRUS cannot be grown, even against a South
facing wall.

♠ Climatic demands alter according to varieties.

Abutilon

There are reputedly over one hundred species of these herbs and shrubs, from the tropical and subtropical regions of the world. Some are vigorous and treelike with wide-open flowers, *A. vitifolium* from Chile is one such with grey hairy leaves and lavender-blue flowers. There is a white form – 'Album' – and another with mauve flowers – 'Veronica Tennant'. Other species such as the Brazilian *A. megapotamicum* are slender-stemmed and best planted against a support facing the sun. This is a curious shrub with neat arrow-shaped leaves and small nodding flowers like red and yellow lanterns.

A third group of hybrids produce large bell-shaped flowers. Among the best are 'Boule de Neige' (white); 'Golden Fleece' (yellow) and 'Royal Scarlet' (red). All are sun lovers and produce their flowers continuously throughout summer and into autumn.

Abutilon × *suntense* 'Jermyns'
one of several hybrids for a sunny position

Acanthus ✳

These stout perennials are found in the wild in Greece and Turkey where they often grow on hot dry hillsides and banks. Most species produce clumps of large striking leaves which are deeply cut or toothed and are excellent when used to break the line of formal borders. They are also most effective when associated with stone urns, low walls and natural rock. *A. spinosus* has beautifully cut leaves, whilst those of *A. mollis* are much broader. Both have tall prickly spikes of flowers which are a charming combination of purple, green and white. They are quite hardy and enjoy sun or shade, though they flower less freely in dark conditions. *A. mollis* is an excellent ground cover, even in shade.

Acanthus mollis
a superb architectural plant

A bold grouping of *Aeonium canariense,* purple *Lantana sellowiana* and grey *Centaurea*

Acacia ✳

Acacia rhetinodes, freely producing rich yellow flowers

Acacia decurrens, fills Mediterranean valleys with gold in winter

The acacias are among the most colourful and popular of all trees in Mediterranean gardens. Several species are so commonly planted that they have escaped and now grow wild in many areas. There are between 700 and 800 species found in tropical and subtropical regions of the world, but only a very few of these are commonly grown in gardens and these mostly from Australia.

The most well known species are *A. decurrens* with green feathery leaves and *A. decurrens dealbata* with silvery leaves. These flower in winter and provide the "mimosa" of the florist. Their great billowy masses of fragrant golden yellow flowers are a feature in many parts of the Mediterranean where they are commonly grown for cut flower.

A. baileyana has smaller leaves which are even more silvery and smaller clusters of bright yellow flowers during winter and early spring. *A. longifolia* and its varieties have willow-like leaves, and so too has *A. rhetinoides* which produces its yellow flower clusters in summer. *A. podalyriifolia* posseses stems and leaves of an intense silvery white.

The acacias are variable in their lime tolerance. *A. decurrens* and *A. d. dealbata* dislike lime in the soil whilst *A. rhetinoides* is reasonably tolerant. They all worship the sun.

Actinidia ✽

Several excellent climbers for the garden are to be found in this group of 40 species from Eastern Asia. The most commonly planted is *A. chinensis* from China whose strong, vigorous stems soon smother walls, fences and archways against which it is planted. Its leaves are bold and heart-shaped and the creamy-white changing to buff-yellow flowers scent the air in late summer, to be followed, on female plants, by bristly, brown, edible fruits which are commonly sold in shops and stores as Chinese gooseberries.

Actinidia chinensis
the female hung with "Chinese Gooseberries"

Aeonium ✿

Aeoniums are striking plants with often large rosettes of boldly overlapping, broad, fleshy leaves. Some species are extremely decorative and are best in walls or among rocks with their rosettes vertical and their roots in well drained soil. They adore the sun and produce, when happy, large crowded heads of yellow star-like flowers during summer.

A. canariense has apple-green flattened rosettes and is found in the wild in the Canary Isles. From Morocco comes *A. arboreum* which bears its rosettes on the branches of a miniature tree. There is a most attractive purple-leaved form of this species.

Aeonium canariense 'Atropurpureum'
ideal for dry walls and sunny banks

Agave attenuata, the Swan-neck Agave with its extraordinary curving flower spike

Agave ✳

The agaves from Mexico and tropical America are one of the most striking and best remembered features of the Mediterranean. This isn't surprising when one considers their huge bold clumps of spine-tipped fleshy leaves curving stiffly from the central core.

A. americana with its blue-grey bloomy leaves is the most commonly cultivated species and has escaped and gone wild in many districts, especially on sea cliffs. There are also several strikingly variegated forms including 'Marginata' with yellow-margined leaves.

A. attenuata the Swan's-neck Agave from Mexico is so called because of its spectacular tall gracefully curving flower spike.

A. franzoninii has leaves of an intense silvery-blue and is very impressive. Eventually the agave sends up a tall pole-like stem up to 6 m. which bears in its upper half, greenish flowers in short branches. Once flowered the main rosette dies but plenty of seed, and often suckers, are produced to continue life. Agaves are important feature plants and may be relied upon to provide a powerful and bold effect especially when planted amongst rocks or on cliffs and steep banks.

Agave surrounded by *Aloes*

Agave americana,
bold clumps of tough spine-toothed leaves

Albizia ✳

Even if they never flowered the albizias would be worth growing for their delightful, deeply divided, feathery leaves. They are large shrubs or small tress from warm regions of the Old World and produce their "bottlebrush" flower clusters in summer or, in the case of the Australian *A. lophantha,* in late winter. Those of the latter are a beautiful sulphur yellow, whilst in the summerflowering *A. julibrissin,* from Asia, they are pink; darker in the form 'Rosea'. Both species are wide-spreading but graceful small trees and should be given plenty of space in which to develop.

Albizia julibrissin 'Rosea'
sporting fluffy flowers above handsome foliage

Albizia julibrissin, 'Rosea'

Aloe ✳

Over 300 species of Aloe are found wild in tropical and South Africa, Madagascar and Arabia. They are shrubby or treelike plants with or without stems. The succulent or leathery stalkless leaves are arranged in spirals or bold rosettes. These are edged with sometimes horny teeth and may be plain green or zoned. The tubular flowers are carried in dense spikes often on long stems and vary in colour from red to orange or yellow, appearing usually during late winter and spring. Aloes require similar conditions to agaves, and these two groups are often planted together to create bold and effective evergreen foliage displays.

Aloe arborescens
bold plants for hot, dry situations

Alpinia ✳

The alpinias are members of the ginger family, in all 250 species native of the warmer regions of Asia and Polynesia. Their bold clumps of large lance-shaped leaves are ornamental in themselves and the tall panicles of nodding flowers come as a bonus in spring or autumn. *A. speciosa* from China and Japan reaches 4 m. in height and bears beautiful orchid-like flowers of white, red and yellow.

Alpinia nutans
a raceme of flowers

Amelanchier ✳

Apart from one species in E. Asia and three others in Europe, the amelanchiers are native of North America. They are deciduous shrubs and small trees, bringing a brilliance to the garden in early spring when their branches are flooded with snow-white flowers. Some species also colour richly in autumn.

A. lamarckii, A. arborea and *A. laevis* are small trees, whilst *A. canadensis* and *A. × spicata* are tall and suckering in habit, forming dense thickets. They grow best in gardens where some moisture is generally available and prefer acid soils.

Amelanchier lamarckii
its masses of
white flowers and new bronze foliage

Ampelopsis ✳

This small group of vines possess tendrils to enable them to climb over supports. They are attractive plants with often elegant foliage and clusters of small but beautifully coloured fruits. One of the most handsome is *A. brevipedunculata* 'Elegans' with leaves mottled and tinted cream and pink and fruits of a striking porcelain-blue.

Ampelopsis brevipedunculata 'Elegans'
in addition to variegated foliage it produces
these attractively coloured fruits

Anthemis○

This group of daisy-flowered annual, biennial and perennial herbs number 200 species in Europe and Western Asia. Many grow wild in the Mediterranean Region, including the yellow flowered perennial *A. tinctoria,* of which there are several garden forms. *A. sancti-johannis* is another attractive perennial, its stems and deeply-cut leaves covered with shaggy grey hair and bearing orange rayed flowers. They love the sun and flower over a long period during summer.

Anthemis
sun loving daisy flowers over a long period

A quiet pool in the garden at Villa Roquebrune

Araucaria ✳

A small group of 18 evergreen trees of which the most familiar in northern gardens is the so called monkey-puzzle, *A.araucana,* from Chile. In Mediterranean regions the Norfolk Island pine *A.heterophylla* and the Bunya Bunya Pine, *A.bidwillii,* from Queensland are more often seen and make beautiful symetrical trees, sometimes of large size.

Araucaria bidwillii, the Bunya Bunya Pine

Arbutus ✳

Up to 20 species of strawberry trees are found in North and Central America, Europe and W. Asia. *A.unedo* grows wild in the Mediterranean Region, whilst *A.andrachne* is native of Greece and S.W. Asia. Both are small, multistemmed, evergreen trees with clusters of small, white, bell-shaped flowers, those of the former in autumn, the latter in late winter or spring. These are followed by small, red fruits. The stems of *A.andrachne* have beautiful cinnamon-red, peeling bark, which is also found in hybrids between the two – *A.* × *andrachnoides.*

These are among the best evergreen trees for hot, dry soils and often develop a charming gnarled appearance in old age.

Arbutus unedo, the strawberry-like fruits follow the white pitcher-shaped flowers

Arctotis○

Arctotis hybrid, with brilliant daisy flowers

Arctotis hybrids, ideal for banks and wall tops in full sun

Among the many lovely flowers from the southern hemisphere these are some of the most spectacular and reliable. There are 65 species in all, annuals as well as perennials, from Australia, Tropical and South Africa, but the most popular species come from the latter country. Many hybrids also exist and all are low growing with large brilliant daisy flowers in a wide range of colours. They are ideal for carpeting dry areas and in return for full sun will fill the summer months with their gay flowers.

Arundo donax ✳

Commonly seen by streams and rivers in the Mediterranean Region, this handsome giant grass has long been popular as a screen or windbreak. Its stout stems produced each spring are clothed with broad greyish-green leaves which rustle delighfully in the wind. A form with broader, more blue-green leaves is 'Macrophylla', whilst 'Variegata' has leaves striped creamy-white.
It is easy to grow in a deep moist soil and quickly forms a tall dense clump.

Arundo donax 'Variegata'
white stripes in regular array

La Garoupe, *Convulvus cneorum* and *Medicago arborea* above the sea

Azara ✿

Eleven species of evergreen trees and shrubs mainly native to South America. These are attractive in their elegant habit and ornamental foliage. All have tiny yellow-stamened flowers – some, like the spring flowering *A. lanceolata* and *A. petiolaris,* in spikes, others in clusters like the summer flowering *A. dentata* and *A. serrata,* whilst those of *A. microphylla* are inconspicuous and hidden beneath the leaves, from which, however, they emit a heady vanilla-like fragrance in late winter. These are happiest on the northern, cooler side of the house.

Azara lanceolata
sprays of yellow flowers in spring

Ballota ✳

Out of the 35 species from Europe and W Asia, only three are commonly cultivated in Mediterranean gardens. *B. frutescens* is a dwarf shrub with spiny flower clusters, whilst *B. acetabulosa* and *B. pseudodictamnus* are grey woolly perennials of charming appearance. All love full sun and a dry soil.

Ballota pseudodictamnus
a useful and attractive dwarf grey sub-shrub

Bamboo ✳

Phyllostachys bambusoides, tall canes maturing to a rich yellow then brown

These woody grasses are mainly native of tropical and subtropical regions of
the world. Those from more temperate regions are popular garden plants in
colder climates. A great number may be found in Mediterranean gardens
where they are useful as screens, lone specimens or ground cover. Their often
tall canes with abundant foliage impart a tropical effect to the landscape and
the sound made by their leaves rustling in a wind is soothing to the ear.
Phyllostachys niger with its polished black canes, is a particular favourite,
whilst the tall clumps produced by the giant bamboo – *Dendrocalamus
giganteus* never fails to amaze visitors from colder more northerly countries.

Beschorneria yuccoides ✿

Beschorneria yuccoides
a bold Mexican plant for a prominent position

Beschorneria yuccoides
striking coral red and green flowers

This splendid plant is one of ten species related to the agaves and all native to Mexico. Bold evergreen clumps of grey-green, sword-shaped leaves eventually give rise to a stout red stem up to 2 m. high, from the end of which bright-green tubular nodding flowers emerge from rose-red bracts in May and June. A most striking plant for a dry soil in full sun. As in the agaves, the main rosette dies after flowering, but sufficient offsetts are produced to continue the life of the colony.

Bougainvillea○

No other plant is perhaps more evocative of the Mediterranean regions than this. Although 18 species are native of South America, it is *B.glabra* and its varieties which are most commonly planted. The long, scrambling, thorny stems soon cover a wall or fence, and when crowded with their deep rose, purple, red or orange flower-clusters, the effect is both stunning and exotic. They are sometimes trained into trees, which they climb with great speed and tumble their glorious stems from the highest branches. The flowers are produced over many months of summer and autumn, making this one of the most popular and reliable of all subtropical climbers.

Bougainvillea glabra
perhaps the most "exotic" of climbers

Buddleia ✳

Over a hundred species of this colourful group of shrubs are known from Eastern Asia. *B.davidii* from China is perhaps the most commonly planted, its long tails of flowers in late summer and autumn attracting butterflies from far and wide. This is an extremely hardy species and Mediterranean gardeners therefore will enjoy even more the charms of the winter-flowering evergreen *B.madagascariensis* with its long panicles of yellow flowers, and the equally effective white *B.asiatica* and creamy-white *B.auriculata* whose flowers fill the winter air with sweet perfume. Many others are available each with its own personal favours.

Buddleia 'West Hill'
a hybrid between *B. davidii* and *B. fallowiana*

Bougainvillea glabra 'Sanderi', an ubiquitous but outstandingly colourful climber

Ornamental Box hedging at Le Clos Fiorentina

Buxus ✳

Although up to 70 species of box exist in the wild, it is the common *B. sempervirens* which we see and plant most often in gardens. This small-leaved evergreen is useful as a hedge or screen, and is amenable to regular clipping as may be deduced from the numerous examples of topiary seen in gardens.

Cacti ✳

It has been estimated that some 2000 species of cacti are found, the majority in the drier regions of South and Central America. Cacti come in all shapes and sizes with or without spines. They are the best plants for hot, dry soils, and several have even escaped from gardens and may be seen apparently wild in the Mediterranean Region. They are usually best when grouped together and associate well with agaves, aloes and similar spiky plants. Of the many kinds planted in gardens, mention might be made of *Opuntia, Cereus, Echinocereus, Xanthocereus* and *Cactus,* members of which provide some of the most interesting and striking of all plantings in Mediterranean gardens.

1 A mixed grouping including, *Echinocactus, Aloe, Aeonium* and *Euphorbia*

2 *Cereus nobilis,* with flowers opening gently from the tops of statuesque plants

3 *Opuntia tunicata* shows most effectively the fierce spines when sunlight shines through

4 *Opuntia,* with both flower and prickly pear fruit

Caesalpinia ✿

As many as a hundred species belong to this group of exotics. They are natives of tropical and subtropical regions of the world and are normally represented in gardens by the Argentinian – Bird-of-Paradise – *C. gilliesii,* and the Japanese *C. japonica,* both extremely vigorous shrubs with long spiny climbing stems and elegant fern-like leaves. The flowers are even more beautiful – yellow with long scarlet stamens borne in tall upright racemes during summer. They are best planted on large walls or allowed to cover old hedges, banks, etc.

Caesalpinia japonica
a large scrambling shrub
for walls and wooden supports

Calliandra ○

This attractive group of evergreen trees and shrubs contains about 100 species native to Madagascar and the warmer zones of Asia and America. Their leaves are deeply divided into fern-like segments, whilst flowers are borne in dense rounded clusters and consist of long colourful stamens. *C. portoricensis* is a shrub with white flower-heads in summer, whilst *C. haematocephala* and *C. fulgens* have red flowers in late winter. They love a hot sunny position.

Calliandra pulcherrima
clusters of brilliantly coloured stamens

Callistemon ✳

The Australian bottle brushes number 25 species and are among the most popular and colourful flowering shrubs from that continent. Several species including *C. citrinus* 'Splendens'; *C. linearis* and *C. speciosus* have, bottle-brush spikes of rich scarlet-stamened flowers in summer, whilst species such as *C. pallidus* have yellow spikes. They love the sun and because of their slender flexible stems make excellent wall shrubs.

Callistemon
with bottle brush
flowers like fire along the stems

Canarina ○

Canarina canariensis is one of three species of herbaceous perennials found in the Canary Isles and Tropical East Africa. It is a small plant to 1.5 m. with vine-shaped leaves and pendant bell-flowers of orange with red veins. These are followed by edible berries. It is sometimes known as *C. campanula*.

Canarina canariensis
an herbaceous perennial too rarely planted

Camellia *

For those whose gardens are situated on an acid soil the beautiful world of the camellia is theirs to explore and enjoy. The glossy evergreen foliage of these shrubs is attractive in itself, but the incredible range of flowers available make the camellia one of the most admired and popular of all winter flowering plants. The varieties of *C.japonica* number in their thousands, whilst those of *C.reticulata* are possibly more exotic in flower.

C. × williamsii is a group of hybrids, one of which, 'Donation', is a favourite wherever it is grown. The flowers of *C.sasanqua*, whilst smaller than most, are usually produced with gay abandon in the Mediterranean sun. For those on alkaline soils camellias may be grown quite successfully in tubs, pots or similar containers, and their only demand is for an abundance of water during the growing season.

Camellia Japonica 'Contessa Lavinia Maggi'

Camellia japonica 'Margharita Caleoni'

Camellia japonica 'Elegans', a well tried cultivar

Camellia japonica 'Kenny'

Cantua○ buxifolia

This small evergreen shrub is one of eleven species found wild in South America. The funnel-shaped flowers are a striking purplish-red with a yellow striped tube and hang from the tips of the arching shoots during spring.

Cantua buxifolia
ideal for wall tops where
its drooping flowers may tumble

Carpenteria✳ californica

This native Californian is a lovely evergreen sun-loving shrub especially when the beautifully shaped white flowers appear in summer. These are shaped like those of a rose with a central cluster of golden stamens adding to the overall effect.

Carpenteria californica
a sun lover from California

53

Cassia ✳

Between 500 and 600 species of *Cassia* are found in the tropics and warm temperate regions of the world. They range from herbs to woody climbers and trees and include two commonly grown shrubs in *C. angustifolia* and *C. corymbosa*. Both require the support of a wall, fence, tree stump or rock and produce in early autumn clusters of bright yellow pea flowers.

Cassia angustifolia
finely-cut leaves and golden yellow flowers

Ceanothus ✳

Over 50 species of *Ceanothus* are found in North America, the majority in California where they occur on hot sunny hillsides and in dry places. Their flowers range from blue to pink and white, but it is the blue flowered kinds which often echo the sky in their intensity. *C. arboreus* is one of the most spectacular when its large evergreen bushes are covered with deep blue flowers in spring. There are many others both evergreen and deciduous, spring as well as autumn flowering.

Ceanothus arboreus 'Trewithen Blue'
one of the most striking of a large group

Cercis ✳

Of the seven species of this group only the Judas tree *C.siliquastrum* is at all commonly cultivated. This native of the Eastern Mediterranean Region is a familiar sight on dry sunny hillsides throughout the Riviera and is a favourite in gardens and parks where it often assumes, with age, an attractive gnarled appearance. The reddish-purple pea flowers flood the branches in spring and are replaced by equally attractive reddish flattened pods.

Cercis siliquastrum
the ever popular Judas Tree of the
Mediterranean

Cercis siliquastrum and *C. s.* 'Alba' carefully trained at Villa Noailles

The feathery plumes of *Cestrum nocturnum* are richly frangrant at night

Cestrum○

Over 140 species of these shrubs are found in the West Indies and warm regions of America, producing their clusters of tubular flowers often over a long period. *C. parqui* is deciduous and bears large panicles of yellow flowers which are fragrant at night. Another species popular because of its night-scented, pale yellow flowers is the evergreen *C. nocturnum* which sweetens the Mediterranean evenings during late summer and autumn. Both *C. purpureum* and *C. × newellii* are tall, vigorous evergreens, the first with reddish-purple, the second with crimson flowers during summer.

Cestrum × newellii
crowded flowers on vigorous shoots

Choisya ✳

A small group of evergreen aromatic shrubs usually represented in gardens by *C. ternata* – the Mexican Orange-blossom. This is an easily-grown shrub, eventually and in ideal conditions forming a dense green mound up to 2 m. high by twice as much across. The clusters of white, sweetly-scented flowers transform the bush in late spring and early summer. Although tolerant of shade it flowers best in a sunny position and because it resents disturbance is best planted when young.

Choisya ternata
masses of orange-scented blossoms

Chrysanthemum ✳

Two hundred species of these daisy-flowered annuals and perennials are found through Europe, Asia, Africa and America. The annual, pale yellow *C. coronarium,* is native to the Mediterranean and is a familiar sight in late summer, often filling fields and roadsides as far as the eye can see. There are several colour shades, all of them make attractive garden subjects. *C. frutescens* is a native of the Canary Isles and is shrubby in habit up to 1 m. Its white or pale yellow flowers are produced almost continuously through the year, a valuable asset.

Chrysanthemum frutescens
a reliable and long-flowering sub-shrub from
the Canary Isles

Citrus ✱

Citrus limonum, the lemon thrives on heat and sun

Few flowers bring back memories of the Mediterranean more clearly than those
of orange blossom. Their delicious scent instantly conjures up scenes
of sun and heat and these conditions are essential to their cultivation. Whether
grown in the open ground or in pots or containers, they bring a
feeling of the sun to the garden or courtyard and indeed reflect the sun's warmth
in their fruits which stud the evergreen leafy branches and fill the markets
in winter. There are some 10 species of *Citrus* and amongst
the most commonly planted in the Mediterranean Region are *C. aurantium* –
the orange, *C. paradisi* – the grape-fruit, *C. aurantiifolia* – the lime, *C. limon* –
the lemon and *C. nobilis* – the Mandarine orange.

Citrus decumana, the Shaddock or Pomelo with its large yellow fruits

Citrus aurantium, an orange tree gnarled and aged

Citrus aurantium, the Orange with its bright heavy fruits

Citrus fortunella margharita, the Kumquat fruit

Cistus ❋

The majority of the 20 species of cistus are native to the Mediterranean Region where they are a familiar and colourful part of the maquis in summer, their evergreen mounds smothered with rose-like flowers of many colours. They are amongst the most reliable and useful shrubs for those making their first gardens.

Cistus × aguilari
large flowers on vigorous plant

Cistus albidus, softens the sharp path edge as it cascades over

Cistus purpureus loves the sunny situations

Clematis ✳

Clematis armandii, a lovely evergreen climber with flowers in spring

Clematis montana rubens, with a profusion of flowers

These are amongst the most popular and desirable of climbers in gardens throughout the temperate regions. Some 250 species are known, most are climbers, and include deciduous as well as evergreen species. Of the evergreens the spring-flowering *C. armandii* is the most often planted, mainly for its sweetly scented white or pink flowers. *C. meyniana* is similar but flowers earlier. Perhaps *C. montana,* especially in its pink variety *rubens,* is the most commonly planted deciduous clematis and is useful for screening and clothing old trees, walls and banks. There are also many beautiful large-flowered hybrids exhibiting a wide range of colours.

Clianthus ○

This is a small group of 2–3 species from Australasia, usually represented in gardens by *C.puniceus* from New Zealand. This evergreen shrub is rather loose in habit and is best when trained against a wall or allowed to tumble from a bank. The peculiar flowers are large and claw-like and are produced in loose pendulous clusters from late summer into winter. In colour they are a brilliant scarlet, though white forms are also known.

Clianthus puniceus
excellent against a wall

Corokia ✳

Six species of these deciduous shrubs are native of New Zealand where they are popular in coastal areas. All have tiny yellow flowers followed by orange or red berries. *C.cotoneaster* become a tangled dome of wiry interlacing branches, whilst C. × *virgata* is taller with erect stems and makes an excellent hedge.

Corokia × *virgata*
tiny star-shaped flowers
followed by orange fruits

Clivia ❋

Only three species of these bulbous plants are known, all from South Africa. *C. miniata* is the most frequently planted, providing bold clumps of evergreen strap-shaped leaves and large umbels of bright-scarlet, yellow-throated, funnel-shaped flowers during spring and summer. It is a most striking plant in flower and makes a useful edging for paths and borders.

Clivia miniata
superb when bordering paths

Convolvulus ✿

The 250 species of this variable group are distributed around the world. *C. cneorum* is a lovely dwarf, silvery-silky shrub producing its pink and white flowers over a long period. *C. tenuissimus* and *C. althaeoides* are trailing shrubs suitable for banks and wall tops. Both have deeply cut and silvery leaves and pale pink flowers during spring and summer. Another excellent species for planting on wall tops is the purple-blue flowered *C. mauritanicus* from North Africa.

Convolvulus cneorum
silvery mounds and pearl-white flowers

Coronilla ✳

Two species of these normally deciduous shrubs are commonly cultivated in Mediterranean gardens. Both are evergreen and both are also found wild in these regions. *C. glauca* is of dense habit with small grey-green leaves and clusters of bright yellow pea-flowers in late winter and spring and intermittently throughout the year. In *C. valentina* the leaves are blue-grey and the flowers deliciously fragrant.

Coronilla glauca
flowers appearing over a long period

Cortaderia ✳

A small group of 15 species of grasses from New Zealand and South America. *C. selloana*, the Pampas grass from Argentina, is the most commonly planted and its large bold clumps of sharp-edged leaves are a familiar sight in gardens in most European countries. The tall, silvery, silky plumes of late summer and autumn are like proud standards fluttering in the breeze. 'Pumila' is a dwarf form, whilst 'Rosea' has pink plumes. 'Rendatleri' has gracefully drooping pink or mauve plumes. They make outstanding groups or specimen plants in lawns and are best isolated rather than planted among shrubs and other plants.

Cortaderia selloana
widely known as 'Pampas grass'

Cornus *

A large group of mainly deciduous trees and shrubs with attractive flowers, fruit, leaves or winter twigs. *C. mas* the cornelian Cherry of southern Europe thrives on any soil and produces its yellow button-like flower-clusters on the naked branches in late winter. These are followed by bright red fruits. It also makes a dense hedge when regularly pruned. *C. nuttallii* from N. America makes a small tree and bears creamy-white flower heads in Spring whilst the Japanese *C. kousa* is generally smaller, with white starlike heads appearing a month later. *C. florida* from N. America has similar flowers ranging in colour from white through pink to rose-red. All three are best suited to an acid soil and enjoy a cool, moist but well drained soil during summer *C. capitata* is similarly inclined though it will take more sun. This species from the Himalaya has sulphur coloured flower-heads in summer and evergreen leaves.

Cornus florida rubra
with attractive rosy bracts
surrounding inconspicuous flowers

Correa ○

These attractive evergreen shrubs number 11 species from Australia and Tasmania. Their small neat leaves are accompanied by pendant clusters of green, white, pink or red tubular flowers during winter. They make excellent hedges and are tolerant of strong winds and sea spray.

Correa backhousiana
one of several species useful as an informal evergreen hedge

Cotoneaster ✳

This important group of deciduous and ever-green shrubs from northern temperate zones provides gardens with a wide range of habits and effects. Evergreen species such as *C. lacteus* and *C. glaucophyllus* make useful hedging and screening subjects, whilst *C. dammeri* and *C. microphyllus* carpet the ground with their prostrate stems and evergreen leaves. The deciduous *C. horizontalis* is another popular low-growing kind. All have white or pink flowers in summer followed by red, orange or occasionally yellow berries which last well into winter.

Cotoneaster × watereri
with its typical profusion of fruits

Cupressus ✳

Up to 20 different species of cypress inhabit the northern hemisphere from Asia to America. The one most commonly seen in the Mediterranean Region is, of course, the Italian cypress – *C. sempervirens* 'Stricta' – whose tall dark columns are a familiar part of the scene and stand sentinel-like by many a house and village. Forming broader, more conical columns is the Arizona cypress *C. glabra,* from southern U.S.A. with foliage of a striking blue-grey. This is equally tolerant of hot and cold climates and is an excellent contrast to the dark evergreens so prevalent in Mediterranean regions. *C. macrocarpa* from the Monterey Peninsular, California, is commonly planted as a screen.

Cupressus sempervirens

An unusual medley of dead bamboo, blue *Ceanothus* and *Hemerocallis*

Cycas ✿

Cycas revoluta, a plant of bold design, member of a primitive family

The cycads are the survivors of a large group of plants which once dominated the earth over 100 million years ago. These strange and arresting plants bear male and female flowers on separate plants and resemble hybrids between ferns and palms. They are in fact more closely related to the conifers. The most frequently seen cycad is *Cycas revoluta* from coastal areas of Japan. Its short, thick trunk and large rosette of dark green, leathery, deeply divided leaves are one of the most striking of all plant effects to be seen in Mediterranean gardens. Often this species forms large dense clumps, and when isolated on a lawn or among rocks, there are few more spectacular sights.

Cyclamen ✳

For sheer colour there are few more breathtaking sights than *Cyclamen persicum* en-mass. This beautiful miniature, the original of the florist's cyclamen, flaunts its pink, purple or white flowers during late winter and spring, and many an orchard becomes a colourful ocean at this time of the year when, in addition, a delicious fragrance is imparted to the clear air. A native of the Eastern Mediterranean, this lovely species is at its best in light shade and flourishes beneath deciduous trees especially. Its leaves are also ornamental, being heart-shaped with a silvery marbled surface.

Cyclamen persicum
the scented wild cyclamen progenitor
of the florist's cyclamen

Cyperus ○

This large and varied group of grass-like perennials (sedges) contains between 500 and 550 species mainly native of the tropics and warm temperate regions. Several species are grown in Mediterranean gardens where they grace streamsides, pools and permanently damp sites. Perhaps the most spectacular is *C. papyrus,* the paper reed of Egypt, whose tall, triangular, jade-green stems, 3–4 m. high bear at their extremities huge spangled globular heads of brown spikelets. The stems of this plant were used to make an ancient writing paper (papyrus). It grows best in shallow water and makes an excellent feature for the small pool.

Cyperus papyrus
a tall handsome reed for waterside

Cyphomandra ☀

There are 30 species of this group from Central and South America and the West Indies. The majority are of little ornamental merit, but *C.betacea* – the so called Tree Tomato from Brazil – is a large shrub which produces edible dark-purple fruits like large plums in spring. These are preceded by bluish-mauve flowers.

Cyphomandra betacea
the tree tomato with colourful and edible fruits

Cytisus ✳

A small group of between 25 and 30 species native of Europe and the Atlantic Islands. The majority of species are hardy and popular in more northerly regions, but several others are only seen at their best in the Mediterranean climate. These include *C.monspessulanus* and *C.maderensis* both with yellow flowers. One of the most ornamental species is *C.battandieri* from the Atlas Mountains of Morocco, whose stems and leaves are silvery silky with hairs. Its golden yellow, pineapple-scented flowers are produced in long dense spikes during summer. It makes a handsome wall shrub when carefully trained.

Cytisus scoparius 'Splendour'
one of many 'Brooms'
to add a splash of colour to the garden

Datura ✿

Datura versicolor, flowers of breathtaking beauty

Over 20 species of these shrubs and annual herbs are native of the tropics and warm temperate regions. Included in this group are the shrubby species of tropical America, often referred to as Brugmansias. These are often large, up to 5 m., and bear large leaves which are softly downy in some species. The glory of these shrubs, however, are their large trumpet-shaped flowers which hang often in great numbers from the branches in late summer and autumn. To see a large specimen in full flower is a wonderful spectacle and almost causes one's heart to miss a beat. Among the most often seen are the fragrant *D.suaveolens* and the similar *D.cornigera,* both with white flowers and both also having double-flowered forms; *D.chlorantha* with fragrant yellow flowers; *D.sanguinea* with smaller orange-red flowers and *D.versicolor* with large flowers which turn from pale green to cream with a beautiful peach suffusion. They are best planted sheltered from winds.

Datura cornigera and its double form ʹKnightiiʹ

Datura sanguinea, soft foliage suspending orange red trumpet flowers

Dimorphotheca○

Seven species of these daisy flowered perennials are native of South Africa and enliven Mediterranean gardens with their sheets of orange, white, pink or yellow satiny flowers which are produced over a very long period during summer. They should be planted where they can tumble down walls or banks and associate well with rocks.

Dimorphotheca
revels in full sun on a bank or wall top

Dimorphotheca jocundum, typical of a reliable group of sun-lovers for banks and wall-tops

Diospyros ✳

Diospyros kaki, its branches in winter studded with colourful tomato-shaped fruits

Although 500 species belong to this important group including the ebony trees, most are unsuitable for Mediterranean gardens. The species most popular in these regions is the Chinese Persimmon or kaki — *D. kaki* — a small deciduous tree with handsome polished leaves, and producing in autumn bright orange-yellow to orange-red edible fruits which are rather like large tomatoes in appearance. These look very colourful and striking on the often leafless branches at this time of the year. The species is dioecious, but female plants whose flowers are unfertilised can produce seedless fruits.

Diplopappus ✿

These dwarf shrubby perennials are often referred to by botanists as Asters. Their finely cut leaves and trailing stems are attractive when allowed to drape over rocks and walls. During winter these become sheets of mauve as the small daisy flowers begin to open.

Diplopappus fruticulosus
a splendid mass of colour during winter

Doryanthes ○

These are bold perennials with rosettes of long, evergreen, sword-shaped leaves. Of the three species, all from Australia, *D. palmeri* is the one most usually seen. This splendid plant produces numerous arching leaves, sometimes as much as 2 m. in length. From out of the rosette in summer rises a stout stem which, on a well established plant, may reach 3–5 m., bearing at its summit a dense conical spike of funnel-shaped deep red flowers. The flowering stems are normally not produced until the plant has reached a considerable size, but the handsome leaves more than make up for their absence.

Doryanthes palmeri
a striking flower
and foliage plant from Australia

Drimys ✳

From the forests of South America comes the
winterbark – *D. winteri* – a small tree with bold
evergreen leaves silvery beneath. The creamy-
white, sweetly scented flowers are produced in
loose clusters in spring. Although wind tolerant it is grown best in a sheltered, semi-shady
site and a moist soil, which is not surprising
considering its native environment.

Drimys winteri
a noble evergreen tree with charming flowers

Echeveria ✳

Approximately 150 species of these succulent
plants are native from southern U.S.A. to
Argentina. Their fleshy leaves, which vary in
colour from green to pink, blue or purple, are
gathered together in striking rosettes. The bell-
shaped yellow, white, orange or scarlet flowers
are born in clusters from a lateral stem. These
plants are excellent in dry positions such as
rocky banks and walls, and associate well with
aeoniums and the smaller aloes.

Echeverias
prefer a sunny bank or a wall top
for their glaucous rosettes

Echium *

Many of the 40 species of echiums are annuals or biennials and common wild plants of Europe, especially the Mediterranean Region. There are, however, a group of biennials and perennial sub-shrubs from the Canary Isles which create a striking effect wherever they are grown due to their large bold rosettes of long hairy leaves and bold dense spikes of blue, mauve or rose flowers. One of the most spectacular is *E. wildpretii,* a biennial whose incredible rose-coloured inflorescences may tower twice the height of a man. *E. descainii* is shorter with blue and white flowers. *E. candicans* and *E. fastuosum* are branched perennials with bold spikes of blue flowers, and there are several hybrids with flowers varying from deep to slatey blue. All look well amongst rocks and on dry banks, flowering in either spring or summer.

Echium candicans, with outstanding blue flowers

Echium and *Wisteria*
bring welcome blue to the garden scene

Echium lusitanicum
erect spikes like coloured candles

Elaeagnus ✳

Some 45 species of oleasters are found in Europe, Asia and North America. Both evergreen and deciduous shrubs occur, one of the best of the latter being *E. angustifolia,* as a large shrub or small tree with narrow, silvery-grey leaves. Of the evergreen species, *E. glabra* and *E. macrophylla,* both from Japan, are useful as informal screens and for covering walls and fences. The latter has attractive silvery, scaly leaves and both will clamber into low trees or shrubs if given the opportunity. All species have small, fragrant, silvery, scaly flowers produced in autumn or spring.

Elaeagnus × ebbingei
a popular evergreen for hedges and screens

Elaeagnus macrophylla, the young leaves are especially pleasing

Eriocephalus ✿

Thirty species of these evergreen aromatic shrubs are native to South Africa. They are often dwarf and associate well with others of a similar habit. Their leaves are covered in white or silvery hairs which form a striking background to the white daisy flowers. *E. lanatus* is one of the best for general planting, flowering in winter and early spring.

Eriocephalus lanatus
dwarf shrub with winter flowers

Erythrina ✿

The Coral trees take their name from the gorgeous red pea-shaped flowers. They are native of tropical and subtropical regions of the world and include shrubs as well as trees in their 100 species. Most commonly planted is the Brazilian *E. crista-galli* which sends up vigorous thorny stems bearing large glaucous trifoliate leaves and ending in long spikes of bright crimson-scarlet waxy flowers in late summer and autumn. It demands a hot dry position and is a spectacular if eventually leggy shrub or tree.

Erythrina christa-galli
thrives in full sun and dry soil

Eucalyptus ✳

Eucalyptus ficifolia,
flowers and foliage useful for flower arranging

Eucalyptus globulus, fast
growing and developing a superb piebald trunk

There are said to be some 500 species of *Eucalyptus* almost all of which are native of Australia. Many species are planted in the Mediterranean regions where they thrive in the warm dry conditions. Their speed of growth is legendary and many are used in forestry and for rapid evergreen screens. *E. globulus,* the Blue Gum, is one of the most commonly planted and in time makes a tree of large dimensions with an attractive bark, peeling away with age in long strips. The white flower clusters are produced over a long period amidst the long lance-shaped leaves. As a juvenile plant it is often used in exotic bedding schemes when its blue-white stems and leaves create a striking effect. Another commonly planted species is *E. ficifolia* whose great clusters of scarlet and crimson flowers make this one of the most spectacular of all flowering evergreen trees. Eucalyptus are normally only grown from seed, and being poor transplanters, should always be planted when very young. Once established they may be allowed to form a normal tree, or, alternatively, may be cut hard back and encouraged to form a large bush of attractive juvenile growths which are useful for cutting for the home.

Eriobotrya japonica, a bold evergreen
tree or shrub

Eriobotrya japonica, the loquat's
handsome fruit

Eriobotrya ❋

E. japonica, the loquat, is one of 30 species of evergreen trees and shrubs from Asia. This
Chinese and Japanese species is a popular and commonly planted bold-leaved shrub producing its sweetly scented, creamy-white flowers in terminal clusters during winter. These are followed by small pale orange or yellow pearshaped fruits which are edible and usually available
from April onwards.

Eupatorium ❋

Some 1200 species of this group are known,
most of which are herbaceous perennials.
Among the few sub-shrubs planted in Mediterranean gardens are the Mexican *E. atrorubens*
with large reddish hairy leaves and bold heads
of purple or mauve flowers during autumn and
winter. Also from Mexico is *E. ianthenum* which
is lower growing with equally large leaves and
large heads of lilac flowers. They love sun but
enjoy a little shade and shelter where conditions
are too hot and exposed.

Eupatorium macrophyllum
colourful in autumn

Euphorbia ✳

This huge group of up to 2,000 species covers an incredible variety of plants including annuals and perennials, herbs, shrubs and succulents. Many kinds are grown in Mediterranean gardens, each adding its own particular effect to the landscape. Amongst the most useful are *E. wulfenii* and *E. characias* both Mediterranean species of evergreen sub-shrub with cylindrical panicles of green or yellowish-green flowers in spring which associate well with stone walls or rocks. *E. mellifera* from the Canary Isles is a bold evergreen shrub forming a large mound of leafy stems and producing honey-scented green flowers in late winter and spring. *E. marginata* is an annual species from North America with striking creamy-white margined leaves and bracts in summer.
From Mexico comes *E. fulgens* with its arching sprays of orange-scarlet flowers, whilst *E. milii splendens (E. splendens)* is a spiny shrub from Madagascar with brilliant scarlet flowers over a long period. Both of these thrive best in a dry rocky soil in full sun, and in some gardens may even be seen self-sown on wall tops. *E. caput-medusa* – the Medusa's Head – from South Africa is a peculiar dwarf succulent plant with thick trailing stems and likewise demands a dry stony soil.

Euphorbia dendroides
a native of the Mediterranean

Euphorbia milii splendens
viciously spiny shrub for dry sunny walls

Exochorda✳

This small group of deciduous shrubs from Asia are useful for their loose elegant habit and their racemes of snow-white flowers during spring. They require shelter from intense heat and will tolerate light shade from deciduous trees.

Exochorda
all have snow-white flowers in spring

Fabiana✳

Fabiana imbricata is an evergreen heather-like shrub of upright habit. It is the most commonly planted of some 25 species which are native to South America and itself originates from Chile. The plumose branches are crowded in spring with small tubular white flowers which, in the variety *violacea,* are mauve or pale purple. It loves a sunny position though not too hot.

Fabiana imbricata
masses of small tubular flowers

Ficus ♠

A huge group of some 800 species of
trees, shrubs and climbers the majority
of which are found in tropical and subtropical regions of the world. They are
extremely variable in habit ranging
from the close carpeting thread-like
growths of *F.pumila* (P. repens) from
eastern Asia to the giant *F.macrophylla*
from Australia. Both are evergreen and
may be seen in Mediterranean gardens
where the former is by far the com-
moner and a very useful small-leaved
creeper for clothing walls and tree
trunks like a miniature ivy. Of the
deciduous species the most commonly
planted of course is the Fig – *Ficus
carica* with its handsome lobed leaves
and edible fruit.

Ficus macrophylla
a giant evergreen fig from Australia

Ficus pumila, soon covering stone surfaces like a miniature ivy

Gazania ❀

Gaziana hybrid, the well-named Treasure Flower of South Africa

These superb colourful daisy flowers equal the *Arctotis* in their brilliance and are well named Treasure flowers. They are low-growing, sun-loving perennials with leaves silvery-white beneath and bear large showy daisy flowers continuously throughout summer. Some 40 species are known, mainly from South Africa, but are most commonly represented in gardens by various hybrids with yellow or orange flowers. They are excellent for planting on dry banks or wall tops where their stems tumble down creating bright splashes over a long period.

Griselinia ❋

Few evergreen trees tolerate wind and sea spray as well as these. Six species are known from South America and New Zealand, but it is *G. littoralis* and *G. lucida,* both from New Zealand, that are commonly planted as a hedge or screen. Their bold yellow-green leathery leaves create a dense wall and when growing in a reasonably moist soil move quickly to form an ideal cover. They are tolerant both of shade and drought when once etablished.

Griselinia littoralis
one of the best evergreen
screens for gardens by the sea

x Halimiocistus ❋

These dwarf evergreen shrubs are hybrids between species of *Cistus* and *Halimium* and offer the same profusion of bright flowers in summer. × *H. ingwersenii* and × *H. sahucii* offer white flowers, whilst those of × *H. wintonensis* have white petals each with a basal stain of crimson-maroon and yellow. Like their parents they love the sun and are excellent on dry banks and wall tops.

× *Halimiocistus wintonensis*
a striking dwarf shrub for full sun

85

Halimium ✿

Native of W. Asia and the Mediterranean Region, these ten species are related to *Cistus* and like them have five-petalled flowers which smile at the sun. They enjoy similar conditions in the garden. Most have yellow flowers, sometimes with a brown or crimson eye, whilst *H.umbellatum* has white flowers.

Halimium lasianthum
bright flowered low growing sun lover

Dimorphotheca ecklonis, fills a clay pot with a mass of daisies

Hedera ❋

Although the ivies are represented by only a
few species in the wild their ranks in gardens
are enormously swelled by the hundreds of
forms, differing in shape and colour of leaf.
They are excellent evergreen carpeters and
climbers, self-clinging except in the so-called
"tree" ivies. The majority have small, various-
ly lobed leaves in green or various combinations of green, white, yellow or pink. They
quickly cover stone or brick surfaces such as
walls and are equally happy on wooden fences
or tree trunks. They are hardy, attractive and
extremely adaptable. Those with large leaves
such as *H. colchica* and *H. helix* 'Hibernica' are
especially desirable, as are the variegated
forms such as *H. colchica* 'Dentata Variegata'
and *H. canariensis* 'Variegata' the latter sometimes known as 'Gloire de Marengo'.

Hedera
one of several large-leaved ivies

Hedera colchica 'Dentata Variegata', a hardy and reliable evergreen cover for walls and banks

Iochroma

There are some 25 species of these attractive trees and shrubs, all native to tropical South America. Their flowers are tubular and range in colour from yellow through blue to red. The most frequently seen species is *I. grandiflora* whose pendulous clusters of flowers are a beautiful rich purple produced in autumn. This is a large shrub and requires warmth and shelter from wind.

Iochroma grandiflora
a rare and desirable colour

Iochroma grandiflora, violet flowers on this fast growing shrub

Jasminum ✳

Jasminum mesneyi, long-flowering jasmine from China

Jasminum polyanthum, a sweetly-fragrant twiner from West China

Few scents flood the mind with memories like that of jasmine. The common scrambling, twining *J. officinale* is popular in most gardens, even those of colder climates, but out of the 300 known species there are many which are seen only at their best in Mediterranean gardens. *J. azoricum, J. polyanthum* and *J. sambac* are particularly attractive and produce showers of sweetly scented white or pink flushed flowers through summer and autumn, and sometimes again in spring. *J. mesnyi* (J. primulinum) is a strong growing evergreen climber with large double yellow flowers in late winter and spring and, like those already mentioned, is ideal for covering walls, fences, bridges, etc.

Kennedia ⌗

Some 15 species of these climbing or creeping evergreens are native of Australia. They provide some of the most reliable and attractive of all vines for Mediterranean gardens. Their pea-shaped flowers are produced in spring and vary from scarlet to blue, purple, rose or almost black, depending on species. Two of the most commonly planted are *K. comptoniana* and *K. ovata,* both of which are sometimes referred to as *Hardenbergia.*

Kennedia comptoniana
one of the most satisfactory
climbers also excellent as a ground cover

Koelreuteria ✳

Koelreuteria integrifolia is a rare species superior to the common species in its larger, glossier leaves and larger panicles of flowers appearing later, in autumn.

Koelreuteria integrifolia
a rare tree with spectacular flowers in autumn

A superb wall of *Jasminum mesneyi* with purple *Lantana sellowiana* below

Kolkwitzia ✳

This easy and hardy shrub was introduced to Western gardens from China by the great plant collector E.H. Wilson. It is known in the United States as the "Beauty Bush", and is well named when the arching branches are wreathed in pink tubular flowers in late spring and early summer.

Kolkwitzia amabilis
well named the Beauty Bush

Lagerstroemia ✳

Although over 50 species are known from Asia and Australia, the *Lagerstroemia* most commonly seen in Mediterranean regions is *L. indica* from China and Korea. This splendid deciduous shrub or small tree develops a smooth trunk with delightfully mottled bark in which the colours grey, pink and cinnamon predominate. The clusters of flower buds are developing at the tips of the shoots during spring and summer and eventually burst open to show their brilliant pink or mauve crimpled petals from late summer into autumn. The flowers are produced even on young plants and there are few colours more striking to the eye.

Lagerstroemia indica
putting on a fine display of colour

Lantana ○

Related to the *Verbena*, these easy to grow shrubs are commonly grown in Mediterranean gardens where they make excellent hedges, especially colourful when in flower. Out of the 150 species known, mainly from tropical regions of America and Africa, the one most commonly planted is *L. camara*, a prickly stemmed shrub producing its rounded heads of pink or yellow flowers over a long period through summer into autumn. These change colour with age and end up orange or red. There are several hybrids with equally colourful flowers. Lower growing and ideal for carpeting dry banks or tumbling from wall tops is *L. sellowiana* whose flowers are rosy-lilac with a yellow eye and are produced continuously through winter.

Lantana sellowiana
a superb trailer for walls and banks

Lavandula ✳

Three species of lavender are normally represented in Mediterranean gardens. *L. pinnata* is perhaps the most frequent perhaps because of its continuous flowering. It forms dense clumps of slender aromatic stems clothed with toothed green leaves, and makes a superb low hedge as long as it is clipped after flowering. *L. stoechas* has deep purple and black flower spikes and grows well on wall tops and dry banks. *L. angustifolia (L. spica)* and its many forms and hybrids is a popular dwarf shrub with gardeners in more northerly climates and has long been grown both for its ornamental and its culinary qualities.

Lavandula pinnata
low mounds of aromatic foliage

Lavatera ✳

A group of some 25 annuals, biennials, perennials and shrubs with often handsome lobed leaves and beautiful mallow flowers in various colours during summer. *L. maritima (L. bicolor)* is a native of the Mediterranean and thrives in the sun. *L. olbia,* especially in its form 'Rosea' is a stout erect shrub with velvety-hairy stems and leaves and rose flowers.

Lavatera maritima
a useful and reliable shrub by the sea

Leonotis ✿

Some 40 species of these shrubs are native to Tropical and South Africa. *L. leonurus* is the one most commonly planted and brightens the autumn with its whorls of bright orange woolly flowers which occur at intervals along the erect, square, grey woolly stems.

Leonotis leonurus
a distinct and colourful shrub
from South Africa

Limonium❋

The flowers of these plants are valued not only for their colour in the garden but also for their everlasting qualities when cut and dried. *L. latifolium* is a broad-leaved perennial with large branched heads of blue flowers. *L. sinuatum,* a Mediterranean native, has flowers ranging in colour from blue to white and rose, whilst the Algerian *L. bonduelii* has yellow flowers. Both are perennials and both are grown commercially in great quantities for sale in markets and florists. Among the annual species, *L. suworowii* from Turkestan produces a long tail-like spike of rosy-lilac flowers. They enjoy full sun and a well drained soil.

Limonium latifolium
flowers are everlasting when dried

Lippia

Lippia citriodora, also known as *Aloysia triphylla,* is the Lemon Verbena, a deciduous shrub or small tree valued for its lemon scented leaves. Its flowers are small, pale lilac and of little ornamental merit. It is often planted in pots or containers enabling it to be positioned by doors or windows on patio or in courtyard where its refreshingly aromatic foliage may be more conveniently appreciated.

Lippia citriodora
the crushed leaves give off
a delicious lemon fragrance

Loropetalum ✳

Related to the witch hazel *(Hamamelis)*, *L.chinense* is a Chinese shrub with small evergreen leaves and masses of white petalled spidery flowers which crowd the branches in late winter and spring. It is an unusual and attractive shrub best grown in a lime-free soil.

Loropetalum chinense
flooded with white spidery flowers in winter

Loropetalum chinense, the spidery flowers crowd the branches in late winter and spring

Lotus ❊

Out of 100 species known for this group, only one is seen with any frequency in Mediterranean gardens. This is *L.berthelotii* from the Canary Islands, a trailing plant suitable for planting in pots, ornamental containers and on wall tops, where its striking blue-green leaves and stems form an ideal backing for the terminal clusters of bright scarlet beak-like flowers from late spring to early summer. Its requirements are full sun and a dry soil.

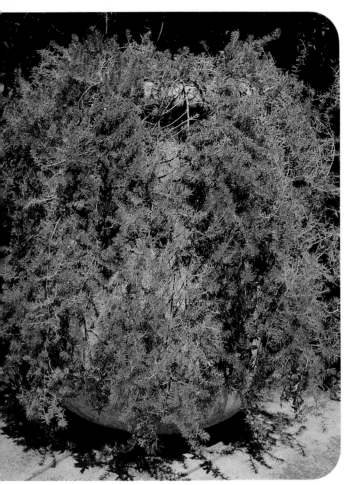

Lotus berthelotii
an enchanting trailer for pots and vases

Mahonia ❊

Several of these evergreen flowering shrubs are popular in gardens of more northerly parts of Europe and all may be used with equal effect in Mediterranean gardens so long as some shade and moisture are always available. The variable *M. aquifolium* is a useful ground cover beneath trees, whilst *M. japonica* from China forms a large spreading shrub with bold foliage and produces long spikes of sweetly scented yellow flowers during winter. Among the choicer species from Eastern Asia are *M. acanthifolia* and *M. lomariifolia* which reach a good size in suitable conditions and begin flowering in autumn. More recently several hybrids of the latter with *M. japonica* have arisen, of which 'Charity' and 'Lionel Fortescue' are two of the best.

Mahonia lomariifolia
handsome in leaf, flower and fruit

97

Magnolia ✳

The members of this large and beautiful group of trees and shrubs may be conveniently divided into those which are evergreen and deciduous. Of the evergreen species the American *M. grandiflora* is perhaps the most commonly planted of all magnolias in Mediterranean regions. Its large glossy leathery leaves form a dense canopy and provide an ideal foil for the equally large fragrant ivory white flowers which are produced continuously through summer and autumn. It makes a striking specimen tree and is adaptable enough to be trained against a high wall. Of similar proportions is the Chinese evergreen *M. delavayi* whose magnificent leaves however are grey-green and dull surfaced. The large parchment-white flowers only last for one day but continue to appear over a long period.

To most people, however, the magnolias most treasured are the deciduous species and few more popular than the Chinese *M. denudata* and its hybrid *M.* × *soulangiana*, of which there are numerous named forms with white or purple-stained goblet-shaped flowers produced before the leaves in spring. These magnolias, however, are best on lime-free soils and require sufficient moisture to supply their considerable needs in the growing season.

Magnolia liliiflora 'Nigra'
a reliable and regular shrub in flower

M. stellata is the Star Magnolia from Japan and makes a large dense twiggy bush covered with star-shaped white or pink flowers in spring. It is a little more tolerant of limy soils than the others mentioned.

Magnolia × *soulangiana*
there are many named forms of this lovely hybrid

Magnolia macrophylla, a large-leaved summer-flowering small tree from the United States. It requires an acid soil and full sun

Melaleuca *

The majority of the 100 or more species of these evergreen trees and shrubs are found in Australia. They are closely related to the bottle brushes *(Callistemon)* and, like them, have brilliant brush-like flower heads made up of dense clusters of stamens. Colours range from yellow to red depending on species, and a tree in full flower presents a breath-taking sight, especially when seen from a distance. They thrive best in a lime-free soil and should be planted when small from pots or containers.

Melaleuca gibbosa
a loose-habited shrub with slender stems

Melianthus *

Melianthus major is one of six species from South Africa and is the one most usually planted in Mediterranean gardens. It is a handsome evergreen foliage plant with large deeply cut leaves of a striking blue-green colour. The brown-crimson flowers are born in dense terminal racemes during summer.

Melianthus major
bold silvery grey foliage when young

Mesembryanthemum ❁

Over a thousand species of this colourful group are known. Those most often grown in Mediterranean gardens are creeping fleshy-leaved perennials, often forming large carpets which, during summer, erupt into brilliant displays of daisy-like flowers. Included in this group are such popular subjects as *Dorotheanthus bellidiflorus* also known as *M.criniflorum* the Livingstone Daisy, which is easily grown annually from seed; *Carpobrotus edulis* – the Hottentot Fig; *Lampranthus* and *Drosanthemum* both of which contain numerous species. All these plants thrive in hot dry positions and are especially effective when tumbling down banks, walls or rocks.

Lampranthus blandus
a useful contrast to the startling *L. spectabilis*

Lampranthus spectabilis, excellent flowering carpeter for wall tops and sunny banks

Musa

Most people know the banana but not everyone is familiar with its tall clumps of long sail-like leaves which bring a tropical effect to the garden. These splendid leaves are very subject to wind and rain damage but are regularly replaced by new leaves emerging from the ground. The huge nodding purple flower head also rises from the ground and emerges from the top of a false "stem" which is formed by the long clasping leaf-stalks. Some 35 species are native of tropical regions and those most often seen in Mediterranean gardens include *M. paradisiaca* and its variety *sapientium*, the latter grown on a large scale in the tropics for its fruits, *M. basjoo* – the Japanese banana, *M. cavendishii* from China and *M. ensete* from Abyssinia.

Musa paradisiaca sapientium
a handsome foliage plant
of great economic importance

Musa paradisiaca sapientum, the incredible
flower heads and "hands" of young fruit

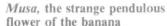

Musa, the strange pendulous
flower of the banana

Myrtus communis tarentina, the prettiest of evergreens for a low hedge

Myrtus ✳

These evergreen trees and shrubs are represented by several species in Mediterranean
gardens. Commonest of all is the myrtle *M.communis* a native of these regions
and a familiar shrub of the maquis. Its small glossy aromatic leaves are
ideal foil for the fragrant white flower clusters in summer and it is an excellent shrub for
sun or shade and will even grow happily by the seas edge. *M.luma* is a small
Chilean tree with beautiful cinnamon and cream mottled stems and masses of white
flowers in late summer, whilst *M.lechlerana,* also from Chile, is darker
stemmed and flowers in spring. Both seed themselves regularly and make useful
informal hedges and screens.

Muehlenbeckia ✳

Two species of this peculiar group of twining
evergreens are commonly cultivated. *M.axil-
laris* is low growing, forming carpets of dense
thread-like stems with tiny rounded leaves.
M.complexa is much more powerful, forming
dense tangles of slender twining stems with
small leaves of variable shape. The latter is an
excellent creeper for covering old fences, tree
stumps, walls, and, if given the opportunity,
will climb into trees, from whence its stems
hang in long curtains. It thrives in shady places
and should not be given too good a position
lest it proves troublesome.

Muehlenbeckia complexa
ingeniously trained to cover a wall with
Jasminum mesneyi in attendance

Nerium ✳

Three species of these evergreen shrubs are known, but the one most commonly cultivated is *N. oleander*, a native of the Eastern Mediterranean Region. The oleander forms a large mound of stiff stems clothed with lanceshaped leathery leaves. During summer and autumn large terminal clusters of brilliant single or double flowers appear in colours ranging from white to pink, purple and crimson. There is even an attractive form with variegated leaves. *N. odorum* from N. India and Japan is similar but with pink single or double flowers which fill the air with fragrance. They are adaptable shrubs and may be grown in pots or containers on the patio or planted as delightul informal hedges. Their main requirements are full sun and plenty of water during spring.

Nerium oleander
thriving in a sunny situation

Olea ✳

The common olive *O. europea* is perhaps the most familiar of all trees in the Mediterranean Region, its leaves giving a grey cast to hillsides and valleys. Many gardens contain olive trees and certainly old specimens can bring a suggestion of antiquity in their gnarled stems and cracked and creviced grey bark.

Olives, *Iris germanica* and *Cyclamen persicum* form a colourful walk

Olearia ✿

Known as daisy bushes in New Zealand where most of the 100 species originate, these evergreen shrubs show a remarkable variety of shapes and effects. The majority produce heads of white daisy-flowers in spring or summer and a few have flowers of blue, lavender or purple. They are among the most reliable and hardy of flowering evergreens and are especially useful in gardens subject to strong winds or sea spray. Several of the taller species make excellent hedges or screens.

Olearia × *scilloniensis*
close up of the numerous daisy flowers

Olearia phlogopappa (purple) and *O.* × *scilloniensis* (white). Crowded with flowers in full sun

Osmanthus ✳

Some 15 species of these evergreen trees and shrubs are native of Asia, many of them hardy enough for cultivation in colder, more northerly climates where they are popular and extensively planted in gardens. *O. fragrans* is a favourite in Mediterranean gardens because of its sweetly scented white flowers in late summer and autumn. It is also known as *Olea fragrans*. There is also a form *aurantiacus* with flowers the colour of chanterelles.

Osmanthus fragrans
sweetly scented flowers in autumn

Osteomeles ✳

A small group of evergreen shrubs often of tangled habit with small, daintily divided leaves. The small clusters of white flowers in summer are followed by red fruits. Without being spectacular these little-known shrubs are satisfying in summer when covered in flower, sometimes appearing as white frothy mounds from a distance. They love a sunny position and a dry soil.

Osteomeles subrotunda
the delicate fern-like leaves
are a pretty foil for the flowers

Palm♠

Without the palms which line her boulevards and stand serenely in her gardens, the Mediterranean would lose much of her charm and character. Several species are commonly planted, of which the Canary Island palm *Phoenix canariensis* is perhaps the one most commonly met with and is a particular favourite for avenues and boulevards. *Trachycarpus fortunei*, the Chusan palm from China, is another popular species. It is also the hardiest palm and may also be found in more inclement northerly climates. Both these palms have green leaves, the former like giant feathers, the latter shaped like rounded fans with fingered margins. *Erythea armata* is normally smaller but makes up for lack of stature with its large strikingly blue-grey fan-shaped leaves, the stalks of which are armed with spines. *Sabal palmetto* the Caribbean cabbage alm and *Livistona australis* from south-east United States are two tall-stemmed fan-leaved species commonly planted in Mediterranean Regions, whilst the Chilean Wine palm – *Jubaea chilensis* is one

Chamaerops humilis
one of the smallest of all palms
and a native of the Mediterranean

of the most impressive palms because of its huge trunk and enormous feather-like leaves.

The only palm native to the Mediterranean is also one of the smallest. *Chamaerops humilis* forms delightful mounds of short stems surmounted by bold heads of fingered, fan-shaped, glossy-green leaves. It is sometimes planted as an informal hedge and is excellent among rocks and on cliffs above the sea.

Erythea armata
the striking blue-grey of the leaves
makes this an unmistakable palm

Phoenix canariensis
the Canary Island Palm
dominating the sky at La Garoupe

Paeonia ✳

Both herbaceous and shrubby peonies are grown in gardens and provide some of the most colourful flowers of all summer. *P. delavayi* and *P. lutea* are mainly grown for their handsome foliage, whilst the varieties of *P. suffruticosa* – the moutan, number over 300. Most of these have been raised in Japan and range in colour from white to yellow, pink and red, both single and double. They grow best in semi-shade and require a rich soil. The herbaceous kinds are also available in a wide range of colours both single and double and are generally of easy cultivation.

Paeonia suffruticosa hybrid
evocative of the East

Persea ○

Of the 150 species of this group, all from tropical regions of the world, only two – *P. borbonia,* the Red Bay from Eastern U.S.A., and *P. americana* the Avocado Pear or Alligator Pear from the West Indies and Mexico – are generally seen in Mediterranean gardens. Both are evergreen trees with dark green leaves, blue-green beneath. Fruits of the former are like small dark blue damsons, whilst those of *P. americana* are the well known avocados sold in shops and markets.

Persea americana
the Avocado Pear presents
a handsome appearance in flower

108

Phlomis ✳

Most travellers in the Mediterranean Regions are familiar with *P. fruticosa* – the Jerusalem Sage – its low domes of erect stems carrying innumerable whorls of yellow two-lipped flowers for months on end in early summer. Sometimes whole hillsides are golden with its presence.

Other species are just as effective and include *P. chrysophylla, P. samia* and *P. longifolia*. Two attractive variations are the pink flowered *P. italica* and *P. purpurea*. All species love the sun and are of great use in new gardens where they will grow amongst rocks or rubble – requiring little or no attention.

Phlomis fructicosa
the Jerusalem sage is
a native of the Mediterranean Region

Photinia ✳

Several evergreen species and hybrids of this ornamental group of trees and shrubs are worth growing in Mediterranean gardens. *P. glabra,* from Japan, makes a large dense bush of dark green leathery foliage which is coppery-red when young. There is also a form called 'Rubens' in which the young growth is brilliant red. It responds well to trimming and makes an excellent hedge. *P. serrulata,* a native of China, is much taller, often a small tree with larger leaves. Hybrids between these two species are known as *P. × fraseri,* and two forms of this cross 'Robusta' and 'Red Robin' are becoming very popular in gardens. Both have bold foliage and bronze-red or coppery-red young growths. They are also suitable for informal hedges or screens and produce flattened heads of white flowers in spring.

Photinia serrulata
a vigorous evergreen
with attractive young foliage

Phylica ✿

A large group of evergreen shrubs mainly found in South Africa. There are several species in cultivation, often dwarf with grey-white or brown downy stems and narrow leaves. Flowers are in heads or spikes in winter and the chief feature are the conspicuous bracts. They are sun lovers and useful on banks and in rocky places, though happiest in lime-free soils.

Phylica ericoides
sun loving shrub for winter effect

Pinus halapensis
the Aleppo Pine acts
as a focul point in the garden

Pinus ✳

Three pines are commonly associated with the Mediterranean Region. *P. halepensis,* the Aleppo pine, is the most frequent, and often forms extensive forest. It is extremely drought resistant and thrives on dry hillsides and cliffs by the sea. As a specimen tree it develops, with age, a dense rounded crown, but crowded specimens often produce tall sinuous stems. *P. pinea,* the Stone pine or Umbrella pine, is very characteristic of the Mediterranean Region, although no one really knows quite where it is native as it is much planted. Its umbrella or parasol-shaped crown is a familiar sight on dry hills and in sandy areas, whilst the large cones contain large edible seeds which are sold in stores. The third Mediterranean pine is *P. pinaster,* the Maritime pine, which, as its common name suggests, is mainly found by the sea especially on sand dunes and in dry gulleys. Its tall majestic stems are reddish-brown and attractively creviced. All three pines are extensively planted in forestry and may be used in larger gardens where their presence often forms the main attraction or the dominant feature.

Pittosporum❧

Pittosporum tobira, sweetly scented flowers
and evergreen leaves

Pittosporum tenuifolium 'Silver Queen' with delightful
creamy-white edged leaves on dainty twigs

This large and variable group of evergreen trees and shrubs offers many suitable subjects for the garden.
P. tobira, from Japan, is commonly planted and seeds itself prolifically once established. Like
many other species it makes a good hedge or screen and is excellent by the sea. Its clusters
of creamy-white flowers during spring and summer fill the air with fragrance. There is also a variegated form.
P. tenuifolium has smaller wavy-edged leaves on black shoots and small deep maroon flowers. There are
also several forms differing mainly in leaf colour and size. *P. adaphniphylloides,* from China,
has large leaves and large terminal clusters of creamy-white, deliciously fragrant flowers, a most handsome
large shrub or small tree. *P. eugenioides* and *P. undulatum,* both with variegated forms, are
handsome and effective small trees in leaf and with sweetly-scented flowers. *P. crassifolium* and
P. ralphii are stiff-habited large shrubs with leathery leaves and dark crimson or purple flowers in spring,
an excellent tough pair for dry or windy sites and very tolerant of sea-spray.
Both also possess variegated forms.

Pistacia *

Ten species of this group are known, occuring in the Mediterranean Region and Asia as well as America. *P. vera* from W. Asia is the Pistachio nut of commerce and is occasionally found in gardens where its bold leathery grey-green leaves are effective. Much more commonly seen are two species native of the Mediterranean Region – *P. terebinthus* and *P. lentiscus*. The former often forms dense low mounds of rich deep green glossy foliage, amongst which the red fruit clusters gleam in autumn. *P. lentiscus* is usually taller and looser growing with larger leaves. Both grow in dry sunny places and are worth planting in such positions in the garden.

Pistacia terebinthus
a common shrub of Mediterranean maquis

Plumbago *

Although 12 species are known from warm regions of the world, it is the South African *P. capensis* which is most usually planted and with which most of us are familiar. There is no other flower quite the same powder-blue, and a large specimen in full flower during summer is a lovely sight. It is a climbing or scandent shrub and needs to be trained against a wall or into a small tree and is sometimes seen as a hedge. It thrives in sun or semi-shade and is very tolerant of heat and drought.

Plumbago capensis
delightful powder-blue flower
over a long period

Prunus ✳

Taken in its broad sense, this important group of trees and shrubs numbers over 400 species including the peaches and almonds *(Amygdalus)*, the plums, cherries and laurels and the bird cherries (Padus). The almond, peach and apricot are grown commercially for their fruits, and whole hillsides are pink with their blossom in late winter and spring. In colder climates they are looked upon as harbingers of spring and wherever they are grown their light shade in summer and early flowering are welcome. The cherries present us with a wealth of exuberant blossom varying from white to rose and fill the garden in late winter and spring with the splendour of the East. A whole group of garden cherries from Japan bring with them a range of shapes, from the narrow columns of 'Amanogawa', to the outflung arms of 'Shimidsu Sakura' and 'Shirofugen'. Although happy on limy soils they are not as tolerant of drought and heat as are the almonds and peaches.

The bird cherries carry their white flowers in long finger-like racemes and bloom later than the true cherries. They are mainly represented in gardens by *P. serotina* and the various forms of *P. padus*. All make sizeable trees and require plenty of space in which to develop.

The laurels – *Prunus laurocerasus* and *P. lusitanica* are evergreen, of robust habit and suitable as hedges and screens. The former is not very happy in limy soils and less tolerant of heat and drought than *P. lusitanica*.

Prunus 'Shirofugen', a beautiful Japanese cherry with wide-spreading branches

Prunus 'Shirofugen'
one of the latest and the loveliest Japanese cherries

Prunus 'Shirotae'
yet another lovely Japanese cherry

Polygala ✳

Between 500 and 600 species of this group are found almost throughout the world. The most commonly planted in Mediterranean gardens include *P. 'Dalmaisiana'* with rose-magenta, pea-shaped flowers; *P. myrtifolia* 'Grandiflora' with rich purple flowers from South Africa, and the erect, slender stemmed,broom-like *P. virgata* also from South Africa with long racemes of purple flowers. All are shrubs and love the sun.

Polygala myrtifolia 'Grandiflora' one of the most floriferous shrubs

Punica ✿

The common Pomegranate – *P. granatum* – is found as a wild plant from S.E. Europe through Western Asia to the West Himalaya. It is, however, extensively planted throughout the Mediterranean Region and is a familiar shrub in flower and fruit. It is a deciduous shrub or a small tree with spiny branches and makes an excellent hedge especially in dry soils. Old specimens often assume a picturesque gnarled appearance and look as old as time itself. The flowers are scarlet with crimpled petals and there are several double forms including 'Flore-pleno' – orange-red; 'Albo-plena' – creamy-white; 'Andre Leroy' – reddish-salmon, the outer petals margined white and 'Spanish Ruby' – ruby-red. There is also a charming dwarf form 'Nana' with single or double flowers which is ideally suited to pot culture. All forms have copper coloured young growths in spring and yellow tints in autumn and are among the most drought tolerant of all shrubs.

Punica granatum, trained as a 'standard' tree helps to show off its scarlet flowers

114

Quercus ✳

Oaks come in all shapes and sizes, both ever-green and deciduous, and can be useful in the garden as dominant keypoints. The evergreen species especially are useful and are also adaptable as hedging, screens or windbreaks. Three species native of the Mediterranean Region are most commonly used including the well known Cork oak – *Quercus suber* – whose rugged corky-barked stems create an appearance of great age and character. *Q. ilex* is even more widely planted and reaches a greater size eventually. Usually seen as a shrub and forming dense and dominant scrub on dry hillsides and garigue is the Kermes oak – *Q. coccifera* – with its small holly-like prickly leaves. This can be used as an effective low hedge.

Quercus suber
the thick corky bark protects
the trunk against excess heat

Rhaphiolepis ❁

A small group of evergreen shrubs producing clusters of white or pink flowers in spring. They are excellent in dry soils and full sun, and may also be trained as low hedges. *R. umbellata* from Japan and Korea has white flowers followed by black fruits, whilst the Chinese *R. indica* is lower growing with white flowers tinged pink in the centre. The loveliest kind however is the hybrid between these two – *R. × delacourii* – which was raised in a garden near Cannes towards the end of last century. It possesses flowers of a beautiful rose-pink, whilst a further selection is 'Coates Crimson' with rose-crimson flowers.

Rhaphiolepis indica
a tough sun-loving evergreen

Romneya ✳

The tree poppies from California are semi-woody plants throwing up annually erect grey shoots clothed with bold, deeply cut, blue-grey leaves. The large white poppy flowers have a bold centre of golden stamens and appear over a very long period during summer and early autumn. They are suckering plants and, once established, soon develop extensive colonies even coming up between paving stones if planted near a path. They love the sun and enjoy dry loose soils and are best treated as herbaceous and cut to the ground each winter.

Romneya × hybrida 'Whitecloud'
glaucous foliage compliments
white poppy like flowers

Rosmarinus ✳

"Rosemary for rememberance" is a common cry, and those who have visited the Mediterranean in spring will certainly remember the pale violet or blue flowers of this small, evergreen, aromatic shrub. The common rosemary is *R. officinalis* of which there are several forms in cultivation differing in habit and flower colour. Another species is *R. lavandulaceus* a more tender plant with prostrate stems which form carpets and is best planted at the top of a wall or bank where its stems can tumble down in close stiff curtains of green and blue.

Rosmarinus officinalis
flanking a flight of steps

Rosa *

Young plant of climbing rose 'Ramona'

The roses need little introduction, being grown wherever gardens are planted and flowers loved. The varieties of Hybrid Tea and Floribunda roses are legion, but it is the wild species from Asia and the numerous old garden hybrids which thrive so well in Mediterranean gardens. These often vigorous shrubs and climbers possess a charm of habit unknown in the popular hybrids and many also present attractive foliage and ornamental fruits as added pleasures. It is perhaps the climbing roses which most attract one's attention with their long stems wreathed with flowers smothering a wall or pergola, or clambering into a tree to tumble down in breathtaking foamy cascades.

R. gigantea 'Cooperi' from the Eastern Himalaya is a favourite with its fragrant white flowers, and *R. brunonii,* the Himalayan Musk, is another rose of similar attributes. *R. filipes* from China is just as powerful in growth and follows its fragrant white flowers with numerous small equally attractive red fruits in autumn. *R. laevigata* also from China is very handsome in leaf and its fragrant white flowers are produced in May and June, whilst its bristly red fruits are a bonus. It is also useful as a ground cover on banks etc., and quickly covers a large area. *R. laevigata* 'Anemonoides' is possibly a hybrid though it resembles the type in most features excepting the soft pink flowers which appear over a very long period. 'Ramona' is similar but possesses striking cerise-crimson flowers. Other roses suitable for covering banks and low walls are *R.* × *paulii* with clove-scented white flowers; *R.* × *polliniana* with pale shell-pink flowers; *R.* 'Max Graf' with fragrant rose-pink flowers over a long period and *R.* 'Raubritter' with semi-double, cup-shaped flowers silvery blush-pink outside and rose inside. High sunny walls provide the ideal support for the Banksian roses – *R. banksiae* and its various forms which bring early blossom in the shape of single or double white or yellow flowers.

Russelia ✿

This peculiar dwarf shrub is useful for planting on wall tops or banks where its rush-like green stems may tumble down. These are enlivened in summer and early autumn by the drooping clusters of tubular scarlet flowers. It is native of Mexico and requires a well drained soil and lots of sun.

Russelia juncea
excellent for a sunny bank or wall top

Santolina ✿

The lavender cottons are a small group of evergreen dwarf shrubs their stems covered with slender green or silvery-grey aromatic leaves. The tiny yellow, white or sulphur coloured flowers are packed into button-like heads at the end of a slender erect stalk and appear through summer. They enjoy a dry sunny position such as a wall top, bank or path-side and should be carefully pruned each year immediately after flowering to prevent an untidy natural habit. They are commonly used in parterres in many Mediterranean gardens.

La Garoupe
the spectacular parterre with grey and green
Santolina, lavender, box and a noble gum tree,
Eucalyptus globulus

Sarcococca ✳

Known as the Christmas Box because of their small leaves and winter flowering, this small group of hardy evergreen shrubs are excellent in shade and are among the few plants able to grow beneath conifers. Their tiny white flower-clusters produce a strong sweet fragrance which pervades the garden on still windless days. Happy in any soil they seem unperturbed by cold or drought.

Sarcococca humilis
forms a useful ground cover in shade

Schinus ✳

S. molle is the pepper tree or Peruvian mastic tree, and is one of the most commonly planted trees in Mediterranean Regions. This is not surprising considering its elegant weeping habit and its tolerance of heat and drought. Its evergreen attractively cut leaves are daintily poised on the long slender branchlets, and the small yellow flowers are born male and female on separate trees. Female trees produce coral-red fruits the size of small peas in summer and autumn. A native of South America, this is a popular avenue tree in cities and towns of Southern Europe, eventually reaching 10 m. or more high. It casts a light shade, ever changing, as its branches are blown in the wind.

Schinus molle
the graceful habit of the Pepper Tree
is popular in warm climates

119

Schizanthus ✳

Sometimes known as butterfly flower or poor man's orchid, the *Schizanthus*
is represented by 15 species all found in Chile. All are annuals
and those most usually grown in gardens belong to either *S.pinnatus* or
S.grahamii or are hybrids of them. Their exquisitely marked and
colourful flowers are born in large terminal clusters in winter and spring,
usually within ten or twelve weeks after sowing. Their fragile stems
require the support of sticks, wire netting or brush-wood to keep them erect.
Planted en-masse they present a sumtuous picture when in bloom and
contrast well with the orange *Nemesia,* another annual.

Schizanthus, a colourful array with *Bergenia* beneath

Scilla ✳

There are said to be 80 species of these bulbous plants though only a relative few are grown in gardens. Late winter and spring is the time when woodlands and rock gardens are blue with drifts of *S. siberica*, *S. bifolia* and *S. amoena*, resembling from a distance pieces of fallen sky. Both *S. italica* and *S. pratensis* open their blue flowers later in spring and are very satisfying to the eye when carpeting the ground beneath trees in wood or orchard. From the Mediterranean Region comes *S. peruviana* with its broad strap-shaped leaves and conical heads of blue flowers in spring. This striking species loves a hot dry position such as wall tops, rocky banks and sea cliffs.

Scilla peruviana
a striking bulb from the Mediterranean

Solandra ⚛

This group of 10 species contains some of the most spectacular of all climbers and shrubs. Perhaps the best of all is *S. maxima* (hartwegii) whose funnel-shaped flowers in spring are from 15 to 20 cm. across. These are a pale cream on first opening but soon turn to yellowish-orange with five dark ribs. It is a native of tropical America and is well worth growing for its exotic flowers which also smell of ripe apricots.

Solandra maxima
a spectacular climber with
flowers smelling of ripe apricots

121

Solanum ✿

Some of the most important of all economic plants are contained in this large group of 1700 species.
There are many weedy annuals also. Fortunately for gardeners, however, there are many shrubs and climbers
of great ornamental merit, several of which flourish and are very popular in Mediterranean gardens.
S. jaminoides from South America is a twining shrub offering showers of pale slate-blue or white yellow
beaked flowers in winter and spring. The Chilean *S. crispum* is herbaceous and annually
produces tall, scandent, hairy, leafy stems which, during spring, are crowded with clusters
of bluish-purple, yellow-beaked flowers. Both species are best trained against walls or through large shrubs
or small trees.
One of the most beautiful species is the climbing *S. wendlandii* from Costa Rica. Its prickleclad
stems allow it to clamber into trees, and so long as it can see the sun it produces showy hanging clusters of large
lilac-blue flowers in late summer. Equally beautiful is *S. rantonnetii* from Paraguay,
a spreading shrub with arching branches bearing, in late summer and autumn, loose clusters
of violet-blue, yellow beaked flowers which are followed by reddish heart-shaped fruits.

Solanum rantonnetii, piles of arching stems studded with yellow-eyed flowers over a long period

Sophora ✿

These deciduous and evergreen shrubs are found in many regions of the world. *S. japonica* - the Pagoda tree from Japan - is a large and noble deciduous tree which produces its panicles of creamy-white flowers in late summer. It thrives in warm dry regions as well as more northerly climes and casts a refreshing shade. From New Zealand comes *S. tetraptera* which, in its various forms, is one of the most colourful natives of those islands. It forms a wide-spreading evergreen shrub or small tree with slender, sometimes weeping, wavy branches, thinly clad with small fern-like leaves. In winter and early spring the whole canopy is strung with drooping clusters of tubular golden yellow flowers.

Sophora tetraptera 'Grandiflora'
the "Kowhai" is
the national flower of New Zealand

Sparmannia ○

africana

Few shrubs are as adaptable to adverse conditions as this South African. Though tender it is commonly used in colder, northern areas where it is a popular pot plant in cafe, office and home. In Mediterranean gardens it is sufficiently hardy to be grown outside in a sunny sheltered position, where its stout hairy stems and large handsome apple-green leaves make a bold feature. The white flowers, with clusters of purple and yellow stamens, are produced during winter and spring.

Sparmannia africana
handsome in leaf and in flower

Spartocytisus ○

nubigenus

Sometimes referred to by the name *Cytisus supranubia,* this striking broom-like shrub from Teneriffe wreaths its smooth green stems with white pea-shaped flowers during spring. It loves a dry sunny position and thrives on rocky banks and wall tops, from which it can tumble its glorious showers.

Spartocytisus nubigenus
the milk white sprays of the Teneriffe Broom

Streptosolen ⚚

jamesonii

This attractive evergreen climber from Colombia is very popular as a greenhouse plant in colder more northerly countries. Its slender twining stems are clothed with rough hairy leaves sticky to the touch. Clusters of brilliant orange tubular flowers are produced during spring and often into summer, at which time this is one of the most striking of all vines. It should be grown against a sunny wall or on a pergola.

Streptosolen jamesonii
brilliant flowers over a long period

Spiraea ❋

Many are the spiraeas which may be grown in Mediterranean gardens.
All are hardy, deciduous shrubs of easy cultivation. In spring the white wands
of *S. thunbergii* and *S. arguta* create snow-like clouds of tiny flowers.
These are accompanied by *S. chamaedryfolia* and *S. prunifolia,* both white
flowered, and later in early summer appear the white foamy masses of
S. nipponica and *S.* × *vanhouttei, S. veitchii, S. trichocarpa* and a host of
others of equal merit. *S. japonica* and its hybrid *S.* × *bumalda* are valuable for
their pink to rose-crimson flower heads during late summer and
early autumn.

Spiraea sp., the white-flowered species gleam in the springtime sun

Strelitzia○

Strelitzia reginae, the beautiful Crane Flower is typical of the "exotic" flora of the Mediterranean

A small group of South African perennials closely related to and in leaf resembling the bananas. *S. reginae* known popularly as the Crane Flower or Bird of Paradise Flower is extremely popular with florists and flower arrangers and makes a superbly refined exotic for Mediterranean gardens with its peculiarly shaped orange and blue flowers emerging from a jade green beak-like sheath. Much more robust is the tall banana-like *S. alba* (*S. augusta*), with its stout "stems", long paddle-like leaves and white flowers. Both species appreciate a warm sheltered position in full sun.

Stylidium *

A large group of interesting plants including several species previously known under the name *Candollea*. These include *S. cuneiformis, S. hugelii* and *S. tetrandra,* all evergreen shrubs from Australia, producing single or terminal clusters of bright yellow flowers during spring. They love the sun and thrive in well drained soils.

Stylidium sp.
sun loving shrubs from Australia

Tamarix *

The many species of Tamarisk are natives of the coastal areas of the northern hemisphere as well as saline soils inland. They are deciduous, mostly large sprawling shrubs with green or grey-green feathery branches becoming plumes of pink or rose in spring or summer *T. parviflora* and *T. tetrandra* are two of the best for spring flower, whilst *T. pentandra* is the most popular summer flowering species.
Tamarisks excell in dry soils especially by the sea and are somteimes planted as hedges or screens.

Tamarix tetrandra
showy plumes in spring

Tecomaria ○

Of the two species belonging to this group only one – *T. capensis* from South Africa – is commonly planted in Mediterranean gardens. Sometimes referred to as *Tecoma* or *Bignonia capensis* this evergreen climber makes a striking low hedge or wall cover with its deeply cut, glossy green leaves and heads of orange-scarlet tubular flowers in late summer and autumn.

Tecomaria capensis
superb over walls fences and balustrades

Teucrium ✳

Several species of this group are grown in gardens. Some are attractive plants for wall tops and rocky banks, whilst *T. fruticans* is an evergreen shrub for dry places in sun or shade. Its stems are white and its leaves grey-green, suitable backing for the small mauve-blue flowers which appear all through summer. It withstands regular clipping and is often used as a low hedge bordering paths, etc.

Teucrium fruticans
slate blue flowers against grey foliage and stems

Thunbergia

Thunbergia gibsonii
richly coloured flowers over a long period

Thunbergia grandiflora
perhaps the loveliest member of a desirable group

Some 200 species of herbaceous plants and shrubs belong to this group, all native
of the tropics. There are several twining or trailing perennials which are popular in
Mediterranean gardens where they are usually trained over pergolas, walls,
fences or banks. Perhaps the most beautiful of these is *T.grandiflora,* a powerful Indian
climber which may even be trained to climb into trees. In late summer
the stems are hung with clusters of blue gloxinialike flowers with yellow throats, which
in their own way are fully as striking as those of a *Wistaria. T.alata* is
native to tropical and South Africa and although much smaller and less ambitious than the
last, has equally striking erect flowers varying in colour from a vivid orange
to white or yellow, with or without a black throat. These are produced
from midsummer into autumn. *T.coccinea* from India is a strong growing climber and
bears pendulous racemes of red flowers during winter, whilst *T.gibsonii* produces
an abundance of rich orange flowers in summer and autumn.

Tropaeolum ✳

There are 90 species of these succulent plants both annual and perennial. The most commonly planted is *T. majus,* an annual fleshy climber or trailer from Peru which, in its numerous colourful forms, is invaluable as a summer ground cover in either sun or shade.

T. peregrinum (canariensis), also from Peru, is an annual climber with neat leaves and pretty yellow flowers throughout summer.

T. tricolorum, a slender, tuberous-rooted climbing perennial nasturtium from Chile with leaves divided into five to seven lobes. The flowers appear at the end of spring. The calyx is red tipped with dark purple and the corolla orange-pink. Semi-shade, cool, acid soil.

Tropaeolum tricolorum

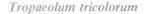

Urginea ✳

A group of some 30 species of which *U. maritima* is a native of the Mediterranean Region. This strange member of the lily family develops a huge bulb from which, in autumn, arises a stout erect stem bearing a long dense spike of white flowers. The large strap-shaped, sea-green leaves do not appear until late autumn and remain through to the following summer. This is a most striking plant, especially when in flower, and is very tolerant of hot dry sites. The bulbs should be available from nurserymen without resort to robbing them from the wild and need to be planted so that the upper part is exposed.

Urginea maritima
tall white fox-tails from huge bulbs

Viburnum ✳

This large and varied group of ornamental shrubs contains many that are admirably suited to conditions in Mediterranean gardens. The most commonly planted, certainly the most useful, is the native evergreen *V. tinus,* which, in its several forms, is ideal for hedges, screens or simply as a specimen bush. The white, pink budded flowers appear through the winter to be replaced by deep blue fruits. There is also an attractive variegated form. *V. odoratissimum* is another evergreen, this time from Malaya, which has striking glossy-green leaves and fragrant white flowers born in large heads.

The evergreen *V. suspensum* from Japan and Formosa also possesses glossy-green leaves up to 13 cm. long and flattened heads of white, rose-tinted flowers in winter and early spring. The attractive red fruits are a bonus. *V. rigidum* resembles *V. tinus* but is larger in all its parts. It comes from the Canary Isles and produces its white flower-heads during late winter and spring. Several deciduous species are also planted, especially the Chinese *V. farreri (fragrans)* and its hybrid *V. × bodnantense,* both of which flood the garden in winter with a sweet fragrance.

Viburnum tinus lucidum, an excellent shrub for Mediterranean gardens. The glossy dark green leaves are ideal backing for the gleaming white flowers

Vitex ✳

Some 250 species of evergreen and deciduous trees and shrubs comprise this interesting group. Only two species however are normally seen in Mediterranean gardens. *V. agnus-castus,* a native of the region, is a deciduous shrub with grey, downy, aromatic stems and deeply divided leaves. The fragrant, pale lavender flowers are carried in long terminal spikes in autumn. *V. negundo* comes from China and is very similar to the last in general appearance. Both are elegant in habit with wide-spreading arching branches. They thrive in dry sunny positions and are very effective when trained against a wall.

Vitex agnus-castus showing the fragrant flowers of this aromatic shrub

131

Wisteria ✳

There are few more exotic climbers than the wisterias with their deeply
divided leaves and gorgeous pendulous racemes of fragrant lilac,
blue, purple, pink or white pea-flowers in spring. Many gardens in the
Mediterranean Region feature these plants, either trained against the wall of
the house or on pergolas, fences, walls and stumps. Sometimes one
sees them clambering into an old tree as they do in their
native forests and there is much to be said for this method of cultivation.
They love the sun and, when trained against or over a support,
require careful pruning to ensure free production of flowering spurs.

Wisteria floribunda 'Macrobotrys', perhaps the most magnificent of hardy flowering climbers

Xanthoceras ✳

This ornamental group contains only two species, both from N. China. *X. sorbifolia* is the one most commonly planted and makes a small deciduous tree, sometimes of rounded habit but more often tall and erect. The white flowers have a dark red eye which later changes to greenish yellow. They are born in short racemes during late spring combining beautifully with the young fresh green, deeply divided leaves. It thrives in full sun and enjoys most well drained soils, even those of a chalky nature.

Xanthoceras sorbifolia
a desirable tree for a sunny position

Zantedeschia ✳

These African perennials all bear arrow-shaped leaves on long erect stalks. The flowers have a characteristic hood (spathe) which is normally coloured and a central poker-like spike (spadix). *Z. aethiopica* is the famous Arum Lily or Lily of the Nile much used in churches at Easter for its pure white spathes. *Z. elliotiana* is smaller with golden-yellow spathes and blotched leaves. They require moist conditions and are best grown at the margin of a pool or stream where they will form colonies in the shallow water.

Zantedeschia aethiopica
the Lily of the Nile in full glory

Yucca ❊

Together with the agaves and the aloes, the yuccas are the commonest and most effective of the bold rosette plants seen in Mediterranean gardens. There are 40 species in all, native of the Southern United States, Mexico and the West Indies, and all produce their evergreen, sword-shaped leaves in handsome, often large tufts or rosettes. Their flowers are normally white and born in erect racemes during late summer and autumn. *Y. gloriosa* is one of the most handsome species developing a short woody trunk at the summit of which the rigid blue-grey, spine-tipped leaves are born in great profusion. From out of the leaves arises a stout branched panicle of ivory white flowers stained purplish brown in bud. *Y. recurvifolia*

is similar but the trunk often branches and the leaves are recurved. Very different in appearance is *Y. guatemalensis* from Central America which attains small tree size with a characteristically swollen base (hence the alternative name *Y. elephantipes*) and several branches each bearing a large cluster of large glossy-green leaves. The large panicles are densely packed with creamy-white flowers, altogether a most striking and ornamental species. *Y. aloifolia* is also tree-like but has blue-grey leaves and flowers earlier. *Y. filamentosa* and *Y. flaccida* are two very popular stemless species. All yuccas demand a dry, sunny position and are excellent for associating with rock or stone-work.

Opposite page : *A colourful corner of the Villa Roquebrune with blue Echium and mauve Diplopappus*

List of additional plants suitable for Mediterranean Gardens

Amaryllis belladonna �	The Belladonna Lily, a beautiful bulbous perennial, the fragrant white, pink to rose-red trumpet-shaped flowers appearing in autumn before the leaves; sun; preferably dry soil.
Aster ✳	A very large group of mainly herbaceous perennials with daisy flowers in many colours. The Kingfisher Daisy - *A. pappei* from S. Africa is a lovely blue flowered species; sun; any soil.
Azalea ✧	Large and varied group of evergreen and deciduous shrubs flowering in a wide range of colours; spring; semi-shade; acid soil.
Baccharis halimifolia ✳	Large deciduous shrub excellent as windbreak; salt tolerant; sun; any soil.
Beaumontia grandiflora ⚸	Climber with twining stems and clusters of large white bell-shaped flowers; sun; any soil.
Berberis ✳	Very large group of evergreen and deciduous, generally thorny, shrubs, attractive in fruit and occasionally in flower and autumn colour good for hedging; sun; any soil.
Brachyglottis repanda ⚸	Large evergreen shrub with bold white-backed leaves and sweetly-scented flowers. Excellent as informal hedge, especially near the sea; sun; any soil.
Canna ✳	Perennials with handsome sometimes coloured leaves and tubular or orchid-like flowers in many rich colours during summer and autumn; sun; any soil.
Ceratonia siliqua ○	The Carob tree, a native of the Mediterranean. Excellent in hot dry positions, a medium sized evergreen tree with leathery leaves and pods; sun; any soil.
Chaenomeles ✳	Small group of deciduous spring flowering shrubs; sun; any soil.

Chorizema ○	Evergreen shrubs with clusters of small but colourful pea-flowers ; sun; any soil.
Cinnamomum camphora ✖	Small handsome evergreen tree with leathery aromatic leaves ; sun; any soil.
Clerodendrum ✳	Deciduous shrubs with purple or white flowers, strong smelling leaves and turquoise fruits ; sun ; any soil.
Cocculus laurifolius ✖	A very ornamental evergreen shrub with vivid dark green leaves. Sun or semi-shade.
Corinocarpus laevigatus ✖	Medium-sized evergreen tree with large leathery leaves and white flowers followed by attractive fruits ; sun ; any soil.
Corylopsis ✳	Deciduous shrubs with clusters of yellow flowers in spring ; sun or semi-shade ; best on acid or neutral soils.
Curtonus ✳	A bold herbaceous perennial with narrow leaves and orange flowers ; sun ; any soil.
Daphne ✳	Evergreen and deciduous shrubs with sweetly scented white, purple or pink flowers in winter or spring; sun ; any soil.
Davidia involucrata ✳	Eventually a large deciduous tree with wide-spreading branches and extraordinary white handkerchief-like flowers in spring ; sun ; any soil.
Dendromecon rigida ✖	Large evergreen shrub best trained against a wall. Poppy-like bright yellow flowers over a long period ; sun ; any soil.
Dipelta ✳	Large deciduous shrubs with pink bell-shaped flowers in spring ; sun ; any soil.
Duranta plumieri ○	Large deciduous shrub with pale purple flowers and yellow berries ; makes excellent hedge ; sun or semi-shade ; any soil.
Enkianthus ✳	Tall shrubs with drooping clusters of small red, yellowish or white flowers in spring ; sun or semi-shade ; acid soil.
Erica ✳	A very large group of evergreen shrubs occasionally tree-like with masses of small flowers in many colours ; sun ; mainly requiring acid soil, but winter-flowering kinds tolerant of limy soils.
Erigeron ✳	Herbaceous perennials with colourful daisy flowers through summer ; sun ; any soil.
Escallonia ✳	Evergreen shrubs with white, pink or red flowers in abundance, good in exposed areas, attractive as hedge ; sun ; any soil.
Feijoa sellowiana ✖	A large evergreen shrub with red and white flowers and edible fruits ; sun ; any soil.
Felicia ✖	A lovely group of long-flowering perennials and annuals mainly from South Africa. *F. amelloides* (Agathaea cœlestis) has blue daisy flowers over low hummocks ; sun ; any soil.

Fendlera ✪	Small to medium-sized deciduous shrubs with pink-tinted white flowers in early summer ; sun ; any soil.
Firmiana simplex ✳	Medium-sized deciduous tree with handsome maple-like leaves ; sun ; any soil.
Forsythia ✳	Small group of hardy shrubs with yellow flowers before the leaves in spring , sun ; any soil.
Fremontodendron ✪	Small group of evergreen shrubs with freely borne yellow cup-shaped flowers over a long period ; sun ; any soil.
Freylinia lanceolata ✳	Evergreen shrub of medium size, fragrant creamy-white or yellowish flowers in late summer ; sun ; any soil.
Fuchsia ✳	Large group of deciduous shrubs with red, purple, pink, white or bicoloured flowers throughout summer ; some are excellent as a hedge ; sun ; any soil.
Gardenia ❋	A large group of up to 250 species of evergreen trees and shrubs mainly from the tropical regions of Asia and Africa. *G. jasminoides* from China and Japan is the most popular and is commonly grown as a pot plant. Its white flowers emit a rich fragrance during late summer and autumn.
Garrya elliptica ✳	Large evergreen shrub, the males with long grey and green drooping catkins in winter ; sun or semi-shade ; any soil.
Grevillea ✪	Evergreen shrubs with crowded narrow leaves and red, pink or yellow flowers throughout summer ; sun ; acid soil.
Hakea ✪	Evergreen shrubs with narrow spine-tipped leaves and clusters of white flowers ; sun ; best on acid or neutral soils.
Hebe ✳	Large group of evergreen shrubs with colourful spikes or clusters of flowers during summer and autumn ; sun ; any soil.
Hedychium gardnerianum ✳	Hardy herbaceous perennial with pleasantly, perfumed spikes of flowers in summer. Lemon-yellow corolla, red stamens. Semi-shade, any soil, though preferably cool conditions.
Heliotropium ❋	Heliotrope, or Cherry Pie, perennials with richly fragrant pale blue to deep blue or purple flowers ; sun ; any soil.
Helleborus ✳	Low growing evergreen or herbaceous perennials with handsome foliage and variously coloured cup or saucer-shaped flowers ; sun or shade ; any soil.
Hesperaloe ✳	Evergreen Yucca-like plants with long, narrow, leathery leaves and slender drooping panicles of red tubular flowers in summer ; sun ; any soil.
Heteromeles arbutifolia ✪	Large evergreen shrub or small tree with heads of white flowers and bright red fruits ; sun ; any soil.
Hoheria ✳	Small evergreen and deciduous trees with clusters of white flowers in summer ; sun ; any soil.
Hydrangea ✳	Large group of deciduous shrubs with conspicuous flattened or globular heads of flowers in many colours during summer and autumn ; sun or semi-shade ; any soil.

Impatiens ✳	A very large group of fleshy annuals, biennials and perennials with colourful flowers in summer and autumn. Many are useful in bedding schemes ; sun or semi-shade ; moist soil.
Ipomea ✳	Large group of mainly twining or creeping herbs with often spectacular trumpet shaped flowers of white, pink, red, blue or purple during summer and autumn ; sun ; any well drained soil.
Iris ✳	Large group of bulbous, tuberous or rhizotomous perennials with grass-like or sword-like leaves and beautiful large flowers in many colours ; sun ; any soil ; some enjoy moist or wet soils.
Jacaranda mimosifolia ⚘	Beautiful small deciduous tree with elegant fern-like leaves and panicles of lavender-blue flowers before the leaves in spring ; sun ; any soil.
Leptospermum ✳	Evergreen shrubs or occasionally small trees with small crowded leaves and small but attractive white, pink, rose or red single or double flowers in summer ; sun ; best in acid or neutral soils.
Lobelia ✳	Annual and perennial plants with striking flowers of many colours ; sun ; any soil.
Lomatia ✳	Small group of evergreen shrubs or small trees with attractive foliage and clusters of cream-coloured or tawny yellow and red flowers ; sun ; acid soil.
Lonicera ✳	Deciduous and evergreen shrubs and climbers many with colourful flowers, sometimes strongly fragrant, followed by red, yellow, black or white berries. Mainly flowering in summer but a few shrubs flower in winter ; sun or semi-shade ; any soil.
Lopezia ✳	Annuals and sub-shrubs with pretty variously coloured flowers in summer ; sun ; any soil.
Malcolmia ✳	Small annuals with variously coloured flowers. *M. maritima* is the night-scented stock ; sun ; any soil.
Mandevilla suaveolens �	Climbing, shrubby tree from Argentina, whose large, white, tubular flowers hang in abundant clusters during the summer, emitting a delicious, jasmine-like fragrance. Full sun, free-draining soil.
Medicago arborea ✳	Evergreen shrub with clusters of small yellow pea-flowers throughout summer. Excellent in sea exposure ; sun ; any soil.
Michelia ✲	Evergreen and deciduous trees with fragrant Magnolia-like flowers in spring or summer ; sun ; acid soil.
Montanoa ⚘	Attractive deciduous shrubs with pink or white daisy-flowers ; sun ; any soil.
Nandina domestica ✳	Evergreen shrub with erect slender stems and large handsome leaves ; flowers white in summer, fruits red ; sun ; any soil.
Othona crassifolia ✲	Carpeting perennial with glaucous leaves and yellow daisy flowers. Excellent on rocky banks and wall tops ; sun ; any soil.
Ozothamnus ✳	Small group of evergreen heath-like shrubs with small clusters of white flowers in abundance ; sun ; any soil.

Parkinsonia ❊	Evergreen and deciduous trees with deeply divided leaves and yellow sweetly-scented flowers ; sun ; any soil.
Passiflora ✳	A large group of mainly tendrilled climbers with unusual and often beautiful flowers ; sun ; any soil.
Phormium ❊	Evergreen plant with handsome sword-shaped leaves and tall branched panicles of tubular yellowish or bronze-red flowers in summer. Excellent in exposed positions ; sun ; any soil.
Phytolacca ○	Several herbaceous perennials for sun or shade and one small deciduous tree for sun. Flowers inconspicuous followed by spikes of dark purple fruits ; any soil.
Piptanthus ✳	Large spreading evergreen shrubs with clusters of yellow pea-flowers in spring ; sun ; any soil.
Pyrus ✳	Small deciduous trees with green or grey leaves and white flowers in late spring ; sun ; any soil.
Ribes ✳	Mainly deciduous but with a few evergreen shrubs and climbers, some with colourful flower-clusters in spring or summer; sun or semi-shade ; any soil.
Ricinus communis ✳	Shrubby plant (may be grown as annual) with attractive foliage (red or purple in some forms) and spicey fruits ; sun ; any soil.
Salvia ✳	Sub-shrubs and herbaceous perennials with aromatic leaves and two-lipped flowers of various colours, often very showy in summer ; sun ; any soil.
Senecio ♠	Evergreen shrubs annuals and perennials with grey or green leaves and heads of yellow daisy flowers in summer; sun; any soil.
Staphylea ✳	Large deciduous shrubs or small spreading trees with usually white, occasionally pink, flowers in spring ; curious inflated fruits; sun or semi-shade ; any soil.
Syringa ✳	The lilacs, a large group of deciduous shrubs with variously coloured, often strongly fragrant, flowers in spring ; sun ; any soil ; excellent on limy soils.
Templetonia retusa ✳	Small Australian shrub with coral-red pea-flowers ; semi-shade ; acid soil.
Trachelospermum ✳	Evergreen self-clinging climbers with twining stems and clusters of sweetly scented Jasmine-like flowers in summer ; sun ; any soil.
Veronica ✳	Herbaceous perennials and alpines with spikes or racemes of blue, pink or white flowers during summer ; sun ; any soil.
Vittadinia ✳	Perennials and sub-shrubs with attractive daisy flowers ; sun ; any soil.
Watsonia ○	Large group of showy montbretia-like perennials with sprays of colourful flowers ; sun ; any soil.
Wigandia caracasana ⚚	Large softly hairy shrub with large handsome leaves and beautiful lilac flowers. Best planted small from pots ; sun ; any soil.

Index

Back cover.
Agave americana silhouetted against the moon's pale glow

Printed in France